HAPPY ENDINGS

by Margaret Logan

Happy Endings

Cover: *Jean Sullivan Design*
Maps: *Richard Widhu*

ISBN: 0-933855-19-2
Library of Congress Catalog Card Number: 99-64865

Published by

PRESS INC.
P.O. Box 156, Liberty Corner, New Jersey 07938

Printed in the United States of America

For T.

One of the greatest happineses of Youth is the Ignorance of Evil, thô it is often the ground of great Indiscretions; and sometimes the active part of Life is over before an honest Mind finds out how one ought to act in such a World as this.

Lady Mary Wortley Montagu
advising on the education
of daughters (1748)

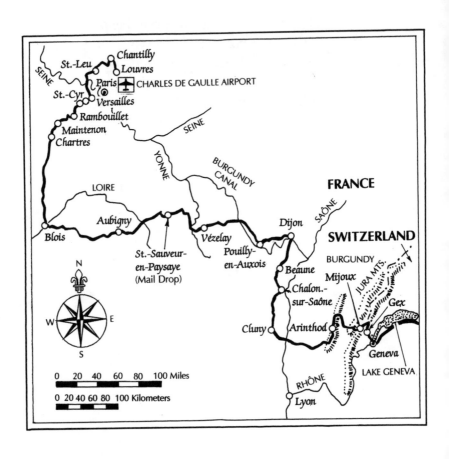

SEINE

St.-Leu · Chantilly
· Louvres

Paris ⊙ ✈ CHARLES DE GAULLE AIRPORT
St.-Cyr
Versailles
Rambouillet
Maintenon
Chartres

SEINE

YONNE

BURGUNDY CANAL

FRANCE

LOIRE

SAÔNE

Aubigny

Dijon

SWITZERLAND

Blois

Vézelay

BURGUNDY

JURA MTS.

St.-Sauveur-
en-Paysaye
(Mail Drop)

Pouilly-
en-Auxois

Mijoux

Gex

Beaune

Chalon.-
sur-Saône

N

Cluny

Arinthod

Geneva

W ⊕ E

LAKE GENEVA

S

RHÔNE

0   20   40   60   80   100 Miles

Lyon

0 20 40 60 80 100 Kilometers

Chapter One

For reasons they keep secret, whooping cranes are not good parents. The mother lays a clutch of two eggs but cannot rouse herself to hatch more than one. The other is squandered unless a light-fingered ornithologist creeps up, claims it, and carries it off to the nest of a sandhill crane.

Sandhills, far more plentiful and adaptable, are terrific parents. Milk and homemade cookies for the whole neighborhood, foundlings, everyone. Quite possibly sandhill foster parents will save the whooping crane from extinction.

A growing number of us—fathers as well as mothers—are like whooping cranes whose children are in the custody of sandhills: teachers, playmates' parents, anyone who'll pick up the slack. Why is no secret. We're in residence, more or less, but emotionally absent; unwilling in marriage, unsettled in divorce, too preoccupied with personal insecurities and failed illusions to give our kids the stability they need. The larger culture, less doubting and tormented, the sandhill culture, fills the vacuum, offering answers and certitude instead of questions behind which lie harder questions.

Ornithologists have a worry about their foster parent program. Is the whooper imprint strong enough to deter pseudo-sandhills from mating with real ones and producing peculiar, even destructive, hybrids? It will be some years before all the answers are in.

My own worry for science is similar: what happens if a whooper, grown to near maturity in the custody of sandhills, runs into her mother in the north-south flyway? Will they have anything to say to each other? It's lonely being a remnant of a dwindling species: the mother, even more than most *femmes d'un certain age*, will be much in need of a real talk with someone who understands. Will she get it?

"No. And you don't deserve to. You reneged. You preferred your own preoccupations, forfeited your chance to mold and influence. And, frankly, you have some nerve to complain. Where would she be if we hadn't stepped in?"

"I'm not complaining, exactly. I appreciate all you've done. But as I get on in years—A daughter, after all—"

"Well, you should have thought of these things sooner. It's too late now. She's happy with us. You, on the other hand, don't look particularly happy—but then, you maladaptive types never do."

Winters my daughter swims competent laps in the serene amnion of a New England boarding school. This summer she has her first real job, baby-sitting for a nice sandhill family in a spiffy part of Cape Cod.

I've borrowed a car to visit her on her day off. We go to the beach, assess the wedge of clouds pushing out of the east, eat a picnic lunch. Discussed are sailboat racing, her new bathing suit, how glad she is to escape the heat back in Boston. Self-centered talk, but what mother of an adolescent would expect otherwise?

Besides, self-centeredness, in your own developing child, is not necessarily boring; the reason I yawn is that I'm obliged to avoid those aspects of her life that fascinate me. I can't, for example, ask her to compare me and her employers, whom she uncritically adores. Nor can I question her taste for vanilla boys.

Vanilla boys are a sandhill subspecies. I (most privately) call them this because they are pale of hair and mien, and because I've theorized that my daughter ends up with them the way people at ice cream counters, bewildered by too much variety, end up with vanilla, pretending it's their favorite flavor.

Is my theory correct? And, rocked in the bosom of sandhill security, does she ever miss the ironies and iconoclasms of whooper life? If I ask, revealing my antisandhill bias, she'll stormily conclude I'm against her; like the shapers of her foster culture, she can't tolerate ambiguity, uncertainty, challenges to accustomed loyalties. Equally stormy for her, and maybe also for me, would be the other side of this coin—the conclusion that she's against me. Only by avoiding troublesome, if intriguing, issues can she keep everything in place, clearly labeled. That is good; this is bad; don't mess with Mister Inbetween. She stands, always, on solid rock.

Nonetheless, since we're so relaxed here on the sand, nothing worrying us but the weather, I will risk, as if idly, a general probe. "What do you think the people around here would be like without their money?"

She gives me a long sideways stare around the thick curtain of her hair.

"I'm talking about substance, of course, not surfaces. Philosophy of life, as we called it before we invented the even flabbier concept of lifestyle. Okay, sorry,"—she hates the verbal games I dote on—"but what effect does money have on people's values?"

"How am I supposed to know?"

"Sort of interesting to speculate, isn't it?"

She rolls onto her stomach, her face away from me. "Not really."

"Why not?"

"It's dumb."

You're dumb, I think, but parents must never call names. Her new bathing suit exposes a slice of vulnerable white skin. Will I put sun lotion there? She won't ask. I won't volunteer.

I yawn again. Boredom is the emotion of restraint. If I drop the restraint and blurt real feelings, by design or carelessly, my daughter's safe, solid rock collapses like sawdust. That even a preoccupied mother retains this awesome power is profoundly disturbing. It's like the national nuclear arsenal: deliberate use is unthinkable. Having such power is horribly expensive. I wish it would vanish, go away. It won't. Sometimes there are accidents, leaks, explosions. Mindful of their destructiveness I watch my tongue, stifle comparisons, edit feelings, yawn.

When the sky is completely overcast we leave the beach. Nothing's left to us but quaintly mullioned shop windows: what the well-dressed upper-income sandhill is wearing this year.

At Lilly's I grow gloomy. Too much hot pink and lime green, colors the sound of hearty summer sailors picking up their moorings at day's end. Too many prints pretending to be audacious but at root only good old Liberty florals shot up with steroids. Too much of the accepted uniform, the expensive and tasteful play uniform.

My daughter emulously craves. She intends to invest heavily at the end-of-season sale. I should come back for it. Fantastic bargains.

This plunges me into despair; why, I don't discover until I'm in sight of Boston's towers. It's not the colors of those clothes, I realize, or even the strange stupidity of dressing expensively for hot-weather play. It's the cut. The assertive, unyielding cut. Those discreet little A-lines are meant to have lives of their own. The planes and dimples of womanly flesh beneath are meant to be superseded, irrelevant.

At their best, sandhills are kind and polite and decorous. These civilized habits, however, are extremely susceptible to tilt. Snobbery is both common and freely permitted. So is frigidity. And my daughter, who'll soon be old enough to investigate life's only adventure reliably worth any price, aspires to a plumage whose stiff geometry satisfies snobbish requirements but will tempt no lover to strip and ravage her.

Some of her remarks come back now. She's loving this summer, just loving it. Her life's goals are clear as never before: ocean frontage and a BMW. "Crammed in between presidential duties at Exxon?" I tease. (Her uncle, long ago, predicted this destiny after observing her adroitly boss some playmates.)

She frowns. "That's one of your ideas. I don't want that. I want this." Her waving arm takes in the entire sandhill enclave—sailboats, lawns, gardens, lounge chairs, privacy, views.

And how will she pay for it without Exxon? Distressingly, the answer to that question is no different in this season of equal opportunity laws than it was in the fifties, when I faced it.

Those clothes she covets are political, strategic, the plumage of the dispassionate merger. Clothes for wives who have married, as they say, for all the wrong reasons. Ahead in the city, cat's-away-mice-will-play summer husbands scamper after women who wouldn't be caught dead in such clothes.

The problem is more serious than I'd thought. More is at stake than having something to say to each other in the north-south flyway. Her boyfriends—the three or four I've met—are not only vanilla colorless, they are invariably, now ominously, rich.

I must do something. Give her an existential shake. Open a chink. Kidnap her, put a new wind in her sails. She thinks she wants everything, but in truth her aspirations are paltry; she wants only the little she's aware of. And she knows no more than I did when, just a few years older than she is now, I ignorantly made choices whose consequences I'm still living with.

That is, I assume she's ignorant. I remember I'd also assumed she'd follow the siren song of equal opportunity. The fact is, I don't know her. I must devise a way to learn her so I can start worrying in a straight line or, reassured, let her be.

Soon after our day together, I have a terrible dream. I have escorted my daughter to the initiation center and am waiting for her in a lounge that resembles a bus station. A dreadful creature, a woman with knobby, thin arms and legs, yellow fright-wig hair, thick brash lipstick, comes to tell me all went well. "She managed her elevations very nicely," is her phrase, which I instantly understand to mean pleasure, orgasm. Then the initiate, eyes downcast, materializes to seat herself, not at my side but next to this creepy functionary. Although she seems shyly content, I am suddenly terrified: the woman's hand is on her thigh, possessively and meaningfully caressing it.

"Sex rears its unpredictable head. So what? Isn't sex what you meant by a new wind in her sails?"

"No! Of course not! What do you take me for? What kind of disgusting and sordid—"

"May we quote you? 'Life's only adventure reliably worth any price.'"

"But my daughter in the hands of that monster!"

"You're hopeless. The one area you claim confidence in and you flunk first time out. All your brave talk of opening chinks and giving shakes—what we've really got here is the blind leading the blind. Hopeless."

That wasn't in the dream; that was the heart-thumping insomniac aftermath.

In the morning, more sanely: middle-class American parents have no institutionalized procedures for their kids' sexual initiation. Directly or indirectly, we help pump them full of expectations of physical bliss, then cover our eyes and ears until someone screams for a shrink or marriage counselor. All our institutions are for after the fact, after the damage is done. Before the fact is disgusting and sordid. Even after the fact, what parents should do is help out with the therapy bills and mind their own business.

Also in the morning, I remember where "wind in her sails" comes from—Henry James's *Portrait of a Lady*. Ralph Touchett, rich and sickly, arranges to give his highly promising, penniless cousin Isabel a fortune—to put some wind in her sails. She, like my daughter, wants everything and knows nothing. Actually, Isabel is more self-assured and ambitious than my daughter; nevertheless, she marries an elegantly vicious and appallingly unworthy husband, an expatriate she encounters in Florence. The book's conclusion is shockingly sad and final. After a kiss "like white lightning" from a lover who hopes to rescue her—the first such kiss in the book and in Isabel's life—she dutifully returns to Italy and the prison her ignorance landed her in.

Well, life doesn't always imitate art, and I am no Madame Merle, the subtle manipulator who set Isabel up for her disastrous marriage. But the book gives me a compelling idea: we'll go to Italy. Henry James first saw Italy when he was twenty-six. It opened and therefore changed his life. In a smaller way, this happened to me in my early thirties. I particularly remember a

Roman afternoon in the Piazza Navona, the October sunlight brilliant on Bernini's fountains. It was abruptly clear to me that if I'd known any of this was here, I'd never have settled so cheap, never.

I will take the kid to Italy next summer. If she still opts for ocean frontage and a BMW, she'll at least have to recognize that she's settling cheap, and this may save her. Illusions and assumptions cause us far more trouble than compromises made with open eyes.

The more I consider this plan, the more I'm excited by the possibility of playing cicerone to this intelligent neophyte, of scribbling lavishly on her every blank page. Such blankness carries an important benefit—few preconceptions will stand between her and the actual experience. At the same time, she won't miss out because I'll be right at her elbow. Her friendly and patient mentor, leading her to see, to feel, to reflect.

A charming picture—except, how patient and friendly am I? And can the guardian of a nuclear arsenal risk the frankness and honesty an effective mentor must? If, at home, snug in our routines, comforts, and distractions, we sometimes have fights that scorch the earth, what will happen among the upheavals and errors normal to travel?

But suppose we start our trip in France instead? She speaks French much better than I, and this will give her an advantage over me, balancing my greater experience. And suppose we travel by bicycle. Granted, I toured northern Italy by bike three years ago, but at her age, with varsity letters in field hockey, squash, and lacrosse, she'll have a decided physical edge. (My God. By summer I'll be forty. The popcult omega. She'll be seventeen, the popcult alpha.)

Including France in this trip represents a small but important motherly sacrifice because I've just been there—two weeks of camping and hitchhiking with the man I've loved so long I can't imagine life without him. Retracing parts of our route will make me lonely for him—and novelty, which sweetens travel's rigors, will be absent for a time. But, like needing to go in the tourist season, it can't be helped. We'll start in France, then, and finish in Rome. A little cycle tour from Paris to Rome.

The Alps. Have to research them. Must be trains. Or hitch on a friendly truck. Time. Forty-five days, for the cheap excursion rate? Have we ever, since she was born, spent forty-five days together? And nights? I don't think so. This could turn out to be less surmountable than the Alps, but the bikes will help; riding along, we'll each have a measure of autonomy, of privacy.

Shuddering, I remember the family vacations of my childhood, all of us trapped in the family car. The upholstery sourly impregnated with the smoke of my mother's incessant Pall Malls. The inevitability that my father would take a wrong turn, that the car would break down. (To this day I can't own a car. It would break down.) The squabbles with my brother, whining "he's on my *side*" until I got slapped. And the horrible awareness that we were doomed to more hours of this than the mind could encompass, that there was no escape, and that any pleasures encountered at our destination would be shadowed by the dreadful necessity of return.

I can spare forty-five days for the trip in the same sense that I can spare the money. I am, occupationally speaking, between engagements, freelancing and oddjobbing. I have money left over from the days when I hid from mothering in full-time work— one of those administrative jobs with a vaunted, greatly overestimated, "creative dimension" that liberal arts majors have to settle for. My odd jobs don't quite cover expenses, and I'll have to go back to real work eventually; taking this trip will simply bring that day closer. We'll be thrifty—picnics and campgrounds or youth hostels. Tipping only for the rare restaurant meal, minimal surface travel costs, no special wardrobe investment, scant temptation to buy souvenirs since every ounce purchased is an ounce to slow us down. Food, our fuel, which we'll burn like gas guzzlers, looks like the sole extravagance.

I phone my daughter to spring the plan. She can't take it in all at once; such a trip, even measured against the stratospheric options routinely entertained at St. Paul's School, has clout. She wants to hang up, bounce the news around, brag, but is stopped cold by a second thought: "Riding all day like that—isn't it just the pits? Don't you get filthy?"

I laugh. Dirt. My exact fear, before that first Italian tour. Worries about stamina, collision, and assault in lonely mountain passes pale before the dominant feminine fear of getting dirty.

"The campgrounds and hostels have showers. But listen— don't you wonder if you can do it? The mountains and all?"

She sounds surprised I'd ask and says no.

"Then how about wondering if I can. Your aged mother."

"But you already did it."

"Not the Alps."

"Well, close enough. And you were alone."

Doesn't she know there are times when alone is easier and more reliable than together? I won't breathe a word, though— this is the time to stress our similarities, not our differences. Our hockey field ruggedness. Our stubbornness that will get us in trouble on this trip as elsewhere, but will also push us over those mountains.

Stubbornness is a characteristic of our sign, Aries. Our birthdays are a week apart.

She wasn't scheduled to be an Aries. After two episodes of false labor, she entered the world three weeks late. We each have a Leo brother exactly twenty months older. Fearful symmetry, is it not? Even the planets struggling to bring me to my mother's attention—though I noticed this particular parallel only after that impenetrable monadnock was dead and gone, and have no idea whether, or how, it struck her.

Those leonine brothers, I then realized, are further alike in their refusal to please anyone until first having pleased their own severe selves. My son, for instance, shook off all custodies at eighteen and hitched out to Alaska where he uncommunicatively seeks his fortune.

Are we alike, my daughter and I? The differences show up more readily. She looks like her father. Her jacket of sandhill manners and loyalties lets her ignore the boredoms and snobberies I rail against and try, sometimes without success, to laugh at. But against this, we do have in common that athletic ruggedness and, best, our physical ease with each other. Despite the years when my passions were focused on myself and motherliness was duty-bound, perfunctory, she never turned into a prickly, aloof, touch-me-not. She demands a full allotment of hugs and backrubs and, big as she is, still climbs into my lap to curl like a baby.

My mother never held me, hugged me, and I knew better than to touch her. She was, as I said, formidably impenetrable. The only thing I ever did that got to her was to give my daughter, right in front of her, the cuddling I had missed.

These scenes had their funny aspect. In silent disapproval, my mother would watch my daughter's nuzzling laminations— the kid, naturally, in this repressive company, required more comforting and cosseting than usual. "That little girl," my mother would say, as if discussing the habits of a remote acquaintance, "is *very* attached to her mama." Her archly European pronunciation of "mama" and an expostulating plume of cigarette smoke were all that gave her away, but for the starving, a crumb is a feast.

I'd have cuddled my daughter anyway, for the sensations, but I won't deny I enjoyed the rest of it, too.

It is spring, the season of our birthdays. My daughter has a glossy, fatly commercial magazine named for this important year. I have something too: I enter what the Massachusetts Commission Against Discrimination calls "the protected group." Prospective employers, when I go out looking for real work, may not ask my age. If they do, or if they guess it and discriminate, a snowstorm of paper work will supposedly redress the injustice.

The alpha and omega of womanly existence.

As it happens, I feel much in need of protection. My good friend, my love, is going willfully, inexorably flat. He claims not to know, any longer, where he ends and I begin; we must separate, not altogether, but enough for him to feel he's living his own life. I've screamed and wept and flung out of rooms—and felt a tap on my shoulder. Right in the middle of hurt and turmoil, I've turned to find a new man suggesting himself.

A fearsome and carefully poised interval follows, for it develops that my old love prefers declaring his independence to pursuing his solitude. I begin to live a double life, which I hate but which tempts me to believe I can change his mind, force outcomes, turn tides. After all, my old love and I have custom going for us, years of tenderness, years of laughter. What will I do to laugh again at our jokes—teach them to this new man? Impossible. I must hold on to what I have.

The situation inspires more bird parallels. The newcomer has to be considered a bird in the bush: he's married. To a sandhill, of course, a vestal virgin of sandhillism who's hanging in for all the wrong reasons, for the BMW, the ocean frontage. Compared to him, then, my old love still seems accessible, a bird in the hand, worth twice as much and guilt-free to boot. Like most women who have been long single, I'm perfectly schooled in reasons for not involving myself with married men.

I will call my old love Adam because he was the first I loved after my divorce. And this new man will be John. Another alpha and omega: Adam's history begins the Bible, John narrates its last Gospel. Is John, then, to be my last love? Having beaten off the insidious concept of Mr. Right, I want no part of this, but the name, for all its portents, sticks. John. It suits him; I'm stuck with it. And Adam.

Am I, no less than John's wife, hanging in with Adam for all the wrong reasons? Some are, at best, peripheral. Company on Thanksgiving and Christmas and other national holidays: can't have that from a married man. Also, Adam secures important indulgences for me from my daughter. She adores him. Her friends adore him. He's a para-parent, old enough to put them on their mettle, but so sportively without portfolio they can treat him as a peer. The cachet he gives my daughter utterly redeems my suspiciously persistent singleness, even to sandhill eyes. He is the modulating graphite of our smoldering nuclear pile. The solemnites of Parents' Day without Adam's editorial snickers in my ear? Never. And how about the mandatory steak 'n' salad bar off-campus "feed" that winds up every proper parental visit? Once, of necessity, I attempted this ritual without Adam. The vanilla boy my invited did his best, but, as she herself later sighed, it just wasn't the same.

Still, a love gone flat is a love gone flat. By way of facing facts, I hint to my daughter that things are not good between Adam and me. She has a fit: Adam can do no wrong. I, however, have a proven record of wrongdoing. She supposes I'm going to take up with some idiot like— —, and she names one of my more outlandish social experiments. "Well, go ahead, do whatever crazy thing you want. But don't make me listen. I don't want to hear anything about it."

The little brat can really hurt. But I don't call her on this selfish, bratty response. I don't remind her I didn't quit until I was laid off, and that being laid off is painful. I don't, finally, say another word, for she's made me aware how much I fear her disapproval. Incredible, but there it unmistakably is: she'll disapprove because I'm sacrificing Adam's good graces for nothing better than someone else's husband. The twerp is my conscience and my common sense, and I'm afraid of her.

Chapter Two

"The obvious solution, of course, would've been Air France," Adam decides on the way out to the airport. "Europeans understand bicycles."

Three different TWA agents have informed me over the phone that bikes must be boxed. The airline has suffered too many damage claims. Boxes are available at TWA for fifteen dollars each—pure robbery, because we're easily under the weight allowance, due to great cleverness in packing.

"Flying Air France doesn't protest the Concorde."

"Ineffectual protest is one thing. Ineffectual protest requiring out-of-pocket expense is quite another."

"Aw *right*," timeworn preppie bray of approval, issues from the back seat where my daughter holds the hand of Blair, her current boyfriend. Our mommy-daddy automotive bickerings are pleasantly nostalgic for her, reassuringly normal, especially in front of Blair.

Blair, clean, polite, clear-skinned, has "been abroad," a tour with his family two years ago. British Isles.

"I was pretty young," he apologized at lunch.

"What did you like best?" I asked, causing Adam's eyebrows to lift humorously. But I've learned: to start a conversation with a sandhill kid, ask the same kinds of absurd questions other adults ask. Anything else confuses them. Anything else from me, that is. Adam can get away with murder.

"Scotland, except for the weather. And the Tower of London."

"The execution post standing in blood-soaked ground?"

"Well, mostly the crown jewels."

Adam's eyebrows again: Yessir, those jewels are real crowd pleasers.

Mine, answering: He's not a boy, he's a cassette. Never too young for the conventional response. Worse, he has no conception of his limits. Ruler of all he surveys. Politely surveys. Rich, too. Häagen-Dazs.

At the terminal, we discover there are no boxes to be had. TWA has been out of them for a couple of years.

Paranoia is the normal humor of an American cyclist, and I suspect the threatened box fee was a ploy to discourage us from bringing our nuisance cargo aboard. My more trusting daughter has taken the airline at its word and worries we'll arrive to find our perfectly tuned and polished machines a mangled mess. "No," I say, because this is what mothers are for, "we're on a lucky streak, remember? It'll be okay." She colors, because the lucky streak announced itself a week ago when one of us got her period early and the other a week late, both in time to be finished by takeoff.

Three other friends show up to say goodbye. One man has a tape measure to record our biceps, calves, and thighs, but he has the wit to see my daughter dislikes this play and leaves her out of it. Blair, too, stands apart from the ribald and rackety grownups. Watching him from the corner of my eye, I think how lunatic my complaints would seem to Ann Landers and her correspondents, coping, as they do, with the loutish, drug-crazed, sociopathic teenage American scene. The friend with the tape measure has also charged me with lunacy—on financial grounds. "Consider your sunset years," was his advice. "Money doesn't buy happiness, but neither will anything else buy it."

Adam kisses my daughter and gives her some last-minute advice. "Always yell at the top of your lungs and in English. It's infinitely more convincing when it's your own language. Scares them more, too."

He hands her over to Blair and kisses me. I detect no regret or yearning in his embrace, even though more than six weeks will separate us. Parting from John was very different, but I can't think of that now. Instead, I send the vanilla boy a thoughtgram: Get what you can while you can. That new wind is going to blow her right by you.

We taxi out, and over the intercom I hear my name. The bikes, my daughter panics, they've fallen out. But it's a delivery, a florist's box, twelve perfect roses, beaded with dewdrops.

We bury our faces in their soft red richness. The cabin crew gathers to admire. These are exceptional roses, apart from the romantic extravagance, botanically exceptional. "Let's eat them," I say to my daughter, a sensualism that makes her blush and, interesting thought, may even have caught her out a little.

"But who sent them?"

"That man I had lunch with yesterday."

Her face closes. Protective of Adam, she'll ask no more questions. But she's mightily impressed—she can't help it.

A surprising man, John. To spare my daughter's loyalties, I'd intended to keep him a secret, but he, apparently, had other ideas. He wanted to make himself known to her, insert himself into our trip, make up for not being the last one to kiss me goodbye. And he wanted to confront us with a delightful problem: what on earth to do with long-stemmed roses when embarking on a bicycle trip?

We decide we'll keep two apiece and distribute the rest around the plane. I head for an attractive man, silver-haired, well-tailored, alone. "Tell you what," he says, as if humoring a child, "why not give them to the ladies?" A man in an aisle seat accepts one from my daughter, whereupon his wife demands, "What about me?" Several go to the stewardesses. An elderly man, French, is beautifully tuned in, applauding both his rose and the motives behind such roses.

Empty-handed, we return to our seats and giggle. We're famous. The whole plane knows about the bicycles.

Every adventure needs a catchphrase, a running joke. Ours comes from our seat-mate, a young, drunk engineer. Though he doesn't speak a word of French, his company has sent him to Paris to deal with a malfunctioning installation. Valves, natural gas—I miss the details. The point is, the necessary adjustments cannot be made. Bitterness sharpens his down-home southern Illinois drawl. He's a straw man on a straw errand, a tossed bone to be chewed in order to buy the company brass some delay. "Why do you think I got so drunk?" he demands in a burst of righteous indignation. Then he loses interest in his problems and moves on to us. "Now let me get this straight," he says. "You two girls are gonna get on your bicycles in Paris, France, and ride them to Rome, Italy. Is that it? Have I got it straight?"

"Right," I say, while my daughter shakes with silent laughter.

"Now don't think for a minute I disapprove," he continues. "But I want to tell you, I'm surprised. I'm not saying there's anything wrong, mind you. But do I have it straight? You two girls—"

(A vision. Weeks later, at dawn in a Swiss pasture, my daughter opens her bluer than Swiss-sky-blue eyes and delivers her line: "Now you two girls are gonna get on your bicycles and ride over those Alps, do I have it straight?")

He's too drunk to notice the years separating us, to guess I'm the mother. But then who am I? "You're not her teacher, I know that. Little old teacher ladies don't get sent roses on airplanes, leastways where I come from they don't." He peers around me to study my daughter, then falls back in his seat laughing. "Lord oh lord. She thinks you're gonna do it all for her. She's gonna let you do the whole thing."

With that strange and chilling prophecy, he leaves us to go wheedle another drink—he's been cut off since Boston. When he returns, my daughter has her arm around my shoulders. His puzzlement is over: clearly, we are lovers. This is, for him, a stimulating idea. He tells me the name of his hotel in Paris. He leans confidentially closer, grows insistent. He can show me things I've never seen, moves I've never tried.

Finally the steward notices my discomfort and coaxes him to a seat at the rear of the plane. We settle into our blankets and sleep.

Futuristic Charles de Gaulle airport is, for us, inconveniently set in farm country northwest of Paris. A superhighway connects it to the city, but since we're skipping the city, we must find a nice, quiet circumferential route.

"All that way," friends have protested, "and you're not even *glancing* at Paris?" Exactly. Paris is not for glancing. My daughter can glance on her own, sneak a weekend from Exxon or any other support system. I will not be a party to such an atrocity.

One has one's standards.

The map we brought, showing only *grandes routes*, is practically useless. What's needed is a Michelin "yellow"; scale, one centimeter to two kilometers. A few false moves and some illegal negotiation of the superhighway allow us to escape the airport complex and find the first sizable town, Louvres. Since I'd stupidly forgotten to get a starting-out ration of French currency in Boston, we must cash a traveler's check before shopping for our yellow.

Catastrophe. It is Pentecost. Bank holiday. Returning to the airport exchange, now that we've set out, is unthinkable, so we forge on to Chantilly where surely a hotel will cash a check. The unreal sensations that accompany all jet travel are magnified; with over a thousand dollars in my pack, we cannot buy a meal. The sun is fierce, but not as fierce as my daughter's scorn. I've utterly betrayed her trust. She thought I knew what I was doing. She keeps inventing new ways to remind me that I let her sleep through breakfast—TWA's orange juice and icy, soggy Danish now burning acid holes in my stomach.

She's too pissed off to speak French, so I'm the one (my accent and ineptitude further fueling her scorn) who discovers Chantilly won't cash a check. I learn, however, that there's a campground ahead at Saint-Leu, a place to sleep until Pentecost is over.

At about six in the evening, faint with hunger, our roses pathetically drooping, we strike the campground. The manager lends us money for supper in town. He, his round young wife, and their baby are so nice we wonder how they can stand working here in this charmless place that's really a low-grade trailer park. We must be the only transients. The regulars, grossly fat, bikini-clad, chat vivaciously in small groups. Children play in the dust. The nearby Oise, presumably a featured attraction, floats a few rowboats and dispirited fishermen on its uninvitingly dirty water. There's a twelfth-century church, but we're too angry with Christianity to go inside, despite the promise of its interesting towers, two Gothic, one Romanesque.

Each diminutive trailer (caravans, they're called) has its own territorial demarcation. Spindly fences enclose delphiniums and marigolds, roses climb too robustly for their frail arbors. One yard, elaborately landscaped with toy windmills and concrete kittens, sports a nameplate: *L'évasion*. My daughter goes rigid. If this is considered escape, what horrors lie at home? How can she survive two weeks, another minute, in a land so demonstrably benighted?

Before we sleep, she sums up the whole wretched day. "I just realized I've never gone hungry before. This is the first time in my life I really haven't had enough to eat." Her voice is full of sober, stunned awareness, as if she's gazing deep into the eyes of steerage passengers disembarking at Ellis Island. For all she knows, the campground at Saint-Leu is "Europe"—a region populated by losers who lacked the gumption to flee to the land of opportunity.

Our tent, designed for one (but not for rain; it won't rain, it can't) and cunningly expanded by me for two, is cramped and hot. The ground beneath us is rocky. Holiday traffic rumbles past ten yards from my head, her toes. I wake often, pursued by sadistic demons wearing cheap scent—but it's only John's roses, flaccid blobs that have worked their way under my nose. What am I doing here? This trip will test my every weakness, all at once. I can't read maps, I'm too old, I can't afford it (the real reason I "forgot" to get francs in Boston or at the airport), I can't put up with this sulky, snobbish kid for six weeks with no one my own age to complain to—

I'm way out on a bad limb and I need protection. I'm sick of playing the brave and sturdy solitary. I'm too old, worn out. But I've blown it. Adam is my last chance for a normal life. I should be spending the summer near him, artfully consolidating my position, insisting on my position, making him love me as I want to be loved. And making him protect me as I need to be protected. Instead, I've climbed out on this limb, clinging foolishly to roses that, for all their initial romantic flash, didn't even last the day. What am I doing? What have I done?

Chapter Three

Disdainful of progress, the whooping crane would rather quit than fight. If human beings elect to replace its beloved wide-ranging water meadows with housing developments and drained tillage, the maladaptive whooper will simply check out.

An appetite for bicycle touring also demonstrates retrograde attitudes towards progress, but while the whooping crane will take no for an answer, I can't—with technology no more readily than with love. So here I am in the morning sunshine, imperiling myself and my child as, inches away, trucks lumber past, their hot and poisonous breath rocking us into wobbly serpentines.

Technocrats believe that progress gives more of us more options, and have scant interest in discussing the unpleasant aspects of their tinkering. They prefer to brag about the richness of a society that offers a choice of, say, driving from Paris to Rome or flying. Technocrats, glued firmly to the cutting edge of progress, regally possess and fluently manipulate its presumed benefits. Since they see only ahead, not behind, they can ignore a critical reality: drivers exercising their choice means bikers must proceed at their own risk.

In *Catch-22*, Yossarian claims the Germans hate him. Told by another soldier that they don't, he asks, "Then why are they trying to kill me?"

It's like this between American drivers and bicyclists, hence the dominant humor of the cyclist, paranoia. The favored compensation is to strike attitudes of moral superiority. We are strong, you are flabby; we are silent and nonpolluting, you are— Tiresome, all of it, wearying in the extreme, and wearying, too, how many cyclists get off on these perversions. They court persecution, confrontation. The rougher the contest becomes, the keener their martyred pleasure.

Though my daughter has been raised to scorn such distortions, she can't yet believe a truck will brake behind her on a narrow village upgrade and match its pace to hers. Instead of holding firm in such situations, she pulls over and slows to a woebegone halt. I tell her she must believe. This is Europe; the bicycle here is still an acknowledged form of transport, with full rights to the road. If we can't believe this, if we signal our skepticism with, say, crash helmets, we might as well give up and rent a car.

Neither of us is used to our baggage yet, the way its weight exaggerates all truck-inspired jitters at the handlebars. And when we stop to consult the map or drink water, our bikes take capricious lunges, scoring our legs with tracks of black chain lubricant, tyro giveaway. (Rubbing alcohol handles these marks, as well as facial road grime, zits, and insect bites. First aid kit in a bottle.)

It's a long way around Paris; if I hadn't been so pure about glancing we could have spent our first night in Versailles instead of our second. Our Pentecostal hunger pangs would have brought history to life, for we're tracing the route of the Paris mob—

women, 6000 strong, demanding bread for their starving children, marching on Louis XVI and Marie Antoinette.

Near Versailles, we hit a mean surprise in the form of a long, steep hill. That mob must have been in good shape if it charged up this monster. We stand on our pedals and pull on our handlebars and wish we had no baggage working against us. I try not to think of the real mountains ahead.

"Look," I call over my shoulder, "an aqueduct!" But she won't look. She hates everything. She dismounts, plods sulkily, dares me to act like anything but a perfectly composed adult. We've been on the road, passing through some pretty scenery (but much more suburban and industrial sprawl) for nine hot, dusty hours.

Three inquiries produce a hotel with a vacancy. I don't care what it costs. The *hôtelier*, interested in our adventure, forgives our filth and shows us where to park our "*chevaux*." He doesn't guess we're Americans until we hand over our passports. He's either pro-American or probicycle; I carry away a pleasant sense that he approves of us as eccentric but chic.

"Us, chic? To a Frenchman?"

"Don't knock it. Remember where blue jeans came from."

Versailles, Chartres, and the chateaux of the Loire, this is our program for the next few days. A neat capsule of cultural significance and lots of flat land to build stamina. I wish geography had allowed us to save Versailles for last so that its stupendousness might strike my daughter more forcibly.

Louis XIV built his palace here and moved the court from Paris so he could spend as much time outdoors as his robust temperament required. To early complaints that there was no town, he serenely predicted that the town would follow the king, and so it did. Now, with the action long returned to Paris, Versailles' heart is a manufactured thing, dependent on the pacemakers and plastic valves of tourism.

Sensitive souls often dislike the palace. It's vulgar, they say, cold and barren. Monstrous. Kenneth Clark, whose urbanity ought to be proof against any attack, has written, "To this day I enter the huge, unfriendly forecourt of Versailles with a mixture of panic and fatigue—as if it were my first day of school."

One reason I wanted to show my daughter Versailles was to test an idea that it will be loved if you permit it to knock you down like a giant wave. Her untutored eyes won't be snagged by detail—she'll be able to experience the whole glorious drench in its entirety. Pausing for detail, at least on a first visit, only aggravates the unhappy suspicion that you are an insignificant speck in the triumphant and gloating vastness, for detail belongs to the human scale and Versailles is superhuman. Louis is not called the Sun King for nothing. The panic and fatigue Lord Clark describes are the bleatings of a besieged ego, and aside from the king's celestial one, Versailles is unconcerned with individual selves. Letting your eye follow the *tapis vert* to the watery infinity of the Grand Canal's horizon is like dropping acid: your ego disappears, just as it's meant to.

And does the kid surrender herself to the giant wave? Not precisely—but then, if surrender to new things were easy for her, we'd be taking this trip for different reasons. She has, however, let go enough to be thoroughly impressed by the palace, and that's enough for me.

After a picnic lunch among the thatched roofs of Marie Antoinette's hamlet, we set off for Chartres, which will be new for both of us.

Place names along our route—Saint-Cyr, Rambouillet, Maintenon—fruitlessly jog my daughter's schoolgirl memory, facts memorized for exams and forgotten. I rummage and recall some material on Madame de Maintenon, that pious beauty who prayerfully bided her time until the king's roving eye was hers (and God's) alone. In history books she's invariably credited with cleaning up Louis' licentious act, but according to Nancy Mitford's witty study in *The Sun King*, her position as mistress and then wife had its drawbacks. No giant waves tempted her— she hated sexual intercourse, and the king, even into his seventies, had at her at least once a day, every day. Court life, war, and hunting, the king's other great pleasures, bored her excruciatingly. She was good with children, unlike the merry Montespan, and raised that earlier royal mistress's many royal bastards.

Her hope and joy was Saint-Cyr, an innovative academy for the daughters of impoverished noblemen who'd otherwise languish meagerly at home or be stuffed into convents and forgotten. Unfortunately, the girls soon drifted away from Madame's ideals of plain living and high thinking and began to dream of making the scene at court. Hallucinations of husbands—princes of the realm—bypassed fiscal realities, for who would want a girl without a dowry? At last Madame was forced to face defeat, drop an iron curtain of conventual repression around Saint-Cyr, and kiss her innovations goodbye. The terrible irony of it was that she'd told the girls time and time again that court ritual was stupid and boring and they were well out of it. If they'd only listened to her, they could have had lifelong access to the simple but free opportunities she'd designed for them.

"But of course kids never listen," I risk. "You don't listen when I tell you there's more to life than ocean frontage and a BMW."

"I knew you were going to say that, I just knew it." But she's laughing. She's in a very good humor. That sprinkle from the great wave has done her good. And we've unmistakably escaped Paris. We're on our way.

*   *   *

The little town of Maintenon appears so suddenly that even at cycling speed we almost miss it. We have to double back and park to properly view the charming chateau planted cozily into its riverine midst.

We enter a green world of wheat fields. The road is narrow and traffic almost nonexistent. A cool, sweet-smelling breeze quarters from the rear. At just the moment that the red sun and the pale gibbous moon hang luminously equidistant above the wide horizon, we sight between these heavenly bodies the piercing spires of Chartres. Exhausted but thrilled, I remember the pilgrims who trekked from Paris to Chartres in the old days of grace and belief. They would have seen, as we did, the holy salients suddenly present.

No one at the hostel seems to care that we've arrived after the official closing time; the place is wide open to the soft night. A new building, it is set into a hillside and has picture windows for the view of the cathedral.

We meet a young Englishwoman with a wicked sunburn who has biked from Paris in one day on a rusty old three-speed. Her gear, stowed in ungainly canvas duffles, must weigh twice ours. She's had two flats and asks us how to repair them without repuncturing. My daughter explains, but we both feel that anyone who has managed so briskly with such an improbable rig— she doesn't even have an athlete's body—should be advising us.

Our mechanical problem is my daughter's real derailleur. She's furious because our bike shop friend at home gave it a clean bill of health, even though she warned him it was no good. "But of course no one believes me. Especially you." True enough. The trouble always occurs on upgrades, which suggests she isn't anticipating enough to shift smoothly. I profoundly hope I'm right, because I'd much rather live with the psychological dimensions of pilot error, touchily defensive though the pilot may be, than mechanical problems beyond my expertise. Every time I hear the tortured rattle of her chain I remember the snapping rear spokes that tarnished my solo trip in Italy. I have new, stronger spokes, but other things can go wrong. With two bikes, twice as much can go wrong, a prospect too daunting to face this early in the game. Blaming her technique is hazardous enough for the time being.

Having settled all that, I imagine the monotonous wrangles to come and, cowardly, reverse myself. It's only money. Next day we'll take the bike to a repair shop.

In careful French, my daughter describes the trouble to Madame. Monsieur is busy in his atelier. Madame will communicate to him that we want a new derailleur. Hang the cost.

Freshly conscientious after this craven episode, I dust off my mentor role for the cathedral. Here, unlike at Versailles, detail is of the essence. "So what do you see?" I brightly quiz after my introductory lecture. "What is it about this structure that makes poets weep?"

"It's big. It's old," she snubs, perhaps the fifth snub of the morning.

"Right. Want to be on your own with it?"

"No, tell me. I'm sorry." She's heard my touchiness and has backed away from confrontation. She's less concerned with information than with humoring me; she guesses I'd like nothing better than to fan up a fight, profaning these Gothic harmonies with a purgative knock-down drag-out row.

I take a deep breath. I will be adult.

Cursorily, she traces motifs, chooses—surprisingly for a kid—the less ornate spire as her favorite. The stained glass is a more decisive hit. The day is cloudy, but if we wait, brief shafts of sun will illuminate what Corbusier calls "the ineffable space" of the nave. ("Ineffable" is too much for her. She'll sit still for stained glass, but sneaked in vocabulary drill goes too far.)

The beatific faces of the kings and queens at the main portal nearly undo me. They seem deeply knowing—but how lightly they wear their knowledge! "Look at them. Their radiance. The *mildness* of their radiance. A graphic, no, plastic representation of grace and faith. They are truly 'full of grace,' don't you think?"

My daughter shrugs, looks blank. Her stiff unresponsiveness successfully pulls the rug out from under my pleasure and leaves me feeling mannered and gushy. "Let's buy the food for lunch," I say coldly.

"If you want."

At lunch accumulated rage boils out of her. "You make me feel totally useless. I *hate* speaking French and you're always setting me up to. You don't trust my mapping. You don't even trust my riding. I'm not having any fun. You keep *peering* at me expecting me to have great big reactions to things just because you do. Well, I don't feel a thing. I look at a statue and I feel nothing. Get it? Nothing. So leave me alone!"

I want to shove the grudging little bitch into the scummy Eure. Pack her home in disgrace. After all I've done— Given her more in one day than my mother gave me in my whole life—

We cry, blow our noses, sit slumped in the leached aftermath. Once the rage has dissipated, the shriveled substance of our quarrel seems too flimsy for credence—but there was nothing flimsy about that rage.

A peace offering, wry: "No one in that hostel thinks you're my mother. You seem too young."

"That's bad. I like to be thought of as your mother."

"How come?"

"I'm proud of you. And besides, it's part of my identity."

"Huh. You don't need me for identity."

"Maybe, maybe not. Do you need me for identity?"

She doesn't answer. At her age, with my own mother, I'd have instantly said yes, meaning, I need to know who you are so I can be your absolute opposite.

What do nearly grown kids need from their parents? Information? Approval? A hidey-hole to snuggle in when the rest of the world does you wrong but to disregard blithely the rest of the time? From her, I'd like approval. A subject too thorny for this tender moment, because the deal sorts out like this: she accepts my adulterous betrayal of her darling Adam, and I'll accept her Blairs, her constricted, wrong-headed snobberies. Clearly, approval will have to wait until we get better cards—or feel better about the ones we're stuck with.

A good bicycle is an assemblage of international components, and bike repair shops tend toward internationally shared qualities. Mechanics in both the United States and Europe work surrounded by a fathomless clutter into which they dive with great precision to pull out necessary parts. All mechanics I've ever dealt with approach a job with breezy competence and a high degree of theatrical flourish. This is probably because even the most exquisitely hand-crafted and fine-tuned racer is, to them, essentially a simple machine that cannot dominate or overwhelm. Improvements in technology, when they come along, are refinements of the intrinsic simplicity, human beings remaining confidently in charge. This benign state of affairs encourages self-expression, theatrics.

Madame tells us our bicycle is ready, but there is the despised derailleur, still in place. Dismayed, my daughter asks why, and Monsieur is summoned. He shuffled rapidly in, wearing broken-down, de-cleated racing shoes, and listens impatiently before interrupting his wife with a torrent of exasperated French. He then slings the bike onto a clamp and, with virtuoso authority, puts it through its paces. Adjustment and lubrication were all that was necessary. But, my daughter worries, will it happen again? Monsieur cannot understand American French, so Madame repeats for him. Another richly gesticulated torrent. He's obviously horrified that we'd consider discarding a perfectly good part. Madame condenses for my daughter: "Perhaps, but he thinks not." To prove his point, he performs further, more intricate demonstrations. Every shift is smooth and silent.

To cover myself completely, I say, let's not fool around, let's just buy a new one. But the kid's convinced and meekly pays up, twenty francs, expensive as European repairs go. On a test run, no complaints. And no one breathes a word about pilot error.

At dinner in the hostel we meet two Californians, an unmarried couple mildly ironical over the unusual amenity of the Chartres hostel—special rooms for married couples—which is not available to them. The woman has biked extensively in mountains—the Canadian Rockies, the Alps. She suggests we forget about biking in Switzerland, describing it as either flat, hot, and dustily truck-defiled or too steeply mountainous for reliable braking. Walking part of the way up, she says, is one thing, but having to walk down after such a climb is a crusher. She launches into an account of losing her brakes in the Rockies and communicates her scare so effectively I'm terror-struck. "Use the Simplon Pass train. Or take trains through the whole country. Switzerland's great for hiking, bad for bikes."

No traveler need ever hunger in vain for free advice. Just as some bicyclists are in it for the paranoia and the moral superiority, some people travel for the deliciously abundant opportunities of advising absolute strangers how to conduct themselves.

But since this woman offers opinions only when pressed, her recommendations carry real weight—for me, at least. My daughter vigorously protests. "If we take the train we won't be two girls getting on our bicycles in Paris, France, and riding them to Rome, Italy."

"It's only a tunnel train under the pass."

"Still."

"Look, I'm afraid of them. There. It's out. I'm afraid of the Alps."

She thinks I'm kidding and swings into her don't-worry-I'll-protect-you number. So as not to spook her, I play along, but the Alps, even here in this wide green plain, have been plucking at the edges of my mind like a huge unpaid bill. Or like a bad tooth that prevents me from biting into the present day with carefree relish.

Actually, there are three bad teeth. The Alps. Tomorrow's encounter with the Loire valley where, last year, in our own time of grace and belief, Adam and I sported as if there were no tomorrow. And an unmetaphorical molar, second from the back, right side; postponed root canal work, could act up at any moment.

These are evening vapors; I should try, such evenings, to remember that exercise clears away vapors, and things always look better when we're on the road. The next day, though it begins inauspiciously with a flat tire, amply proves this.

We ride through endless stretches of gray-green wheat and golden barley, the barley like heaped spun sugar, gleaming in the sun, whiskery and top-heavily ripe. Roses climb every stone wall, every fence. The air is wonderfully clean and sweet, and for relief from the sun, we have the forest of Citeaux, purple foxgloves clustering in cool green shade.

"Mom? I don't mean this to be bratty, but why are we doing

this? To say we have, or to prove we can?"

I laugh because she's hit on a central, though furtive, truth of travel—its charm is just as likely to be retrospective as immediate. "Travel is one of life's great experiences," I say. "People slave all year at jobs they hate so they can travel on their vacations. And so they'll have something to talk about afterwards, leaving out the boring parts."

"We won't have any boring parts."

"How about going on and on like this?" If we make Blois, as planned, we'll have managed a hundred twenty kilometers today. My previous record is a hundred. (We always reckon in kilometers, the larger figures pacifying our American compulsion to pile up the mileage.)

"It's okay. I like it. I like riding better than sightseeing."

"Not so many fights."

"I still don't see how you did it alone."

"Alone you're less ambitious. Shorter stretches."

"No one's egging you on, so you can be lazy?"

I laugh again. Two significant travel truths in one day—not bad for seventeen.

Chapter *Four*

In the campground at Blois, we're forced to pitch our tent morbidly close to the spot where, one morning last summer, Adam and I, cramped but unhurried, waited out a rainstorm. I flee to the shower, appropriately cold and rectifying.

Clean, wearing our clean town clothes, we walk across the Loire toward the chateau, batting thick clouds of tiny white moths away from our faces.

"If you have one moth ball in this hand," my daughter says, "and another moth ball in this hand, what do you have?" Her hands, palm up, are about a foot apart.

"I give up."

"A hell of a big moth."

The first dirty joke she's ever told me.

We find a sidewalk café and wait under the brilliant pink sky for darkness. We're attending the *son et lumière*, a first for us both. I bet we fall asleep.

In the lovely inner court of the chateau, next to Francis the First's artfully airy staircase, we spot the young Englishwoman from Chartres. She has had no more punctures, she tells us, and goes on to say her final destination is Tours, where she'll join an archaeological dig. Feeling as if we're old friends, I'd like to swap road stories with her, but she's escorted by a compatriot she seems interested in protecting from our scrutiny.

He's a weedy one, with a hatchet face and dressed all in black—windbreaker, loafers, slacks. We sit behind them and eavesdrop, another kind of fun. "So they put it to me," she concludes in a clear, carrying voice, "either go off the pill or go off your contacts." He squirms appreciatively. "Ew new thets mewst intrestin," he says, and begs for more. He seems, in his rusty black, altogether too sleazy and unprepossessing to know, first-hand, about the pill or any other womanly thing. If he had her looks and she his, he'd never even notice her. Women are amazing. Make an effort for anyone. (John used to argue this point with me, until I vanquished him utterly. "Who did Henry Kissinger use to date in his movie star phase? Okay, and how many times have you seen Golda Meir on the arm of Robert Redford?")

The *son et lumière*, focusing on the famous women of Blois, offers this refrain: "The spirit moves and time does not know its shape. Who better than a woman to breathe life into the unliving?" My daughter cracks up every time she hears it, which is often. Joan of Arc slept here. Then the queens—Anne of Brittany, Claude of France, Catherine de Medici. Claude, an austere, modest woman, is made to seem a ninny: "Do you love your little Claude less than war, my Lord?" Catherine suffered terrible nightmares (the *lumière* flashes red in her rooms) about the violent deaths awaiting her sons. She is treated, for a figure so problematic, sympathetically. Not so Diane de Poitiers, her sublime rival. Well, that's the way the world is. If you like the wife, you take a position against the mistress.

"When I grow up," I announce as we walk back to the campground, "I want to be Diane de Poitiers," but the kid's either too sleepy to care why or too young to appreciate a pisser who lasted well into her sixties.

Throughout chateau country—at Chaumont, Chambord, Chenonceaux, Blois—the initials of Diane and Henry II, king of France, are perpetually intertwined. Their love lasted nearly thirty years, a statistic further enhanced by her being eighteen years his senior.

Catherine de Medici, Henry's queen, bore the situation and bore also ten children, some slightly mad and three to become French kings. Catherine did triumph at Chenonceaux: partisan as I am, I admit her long gallery over the river is brilliant and her garden surpasses Diane's—but then, she was Italian, and that accounts for everything in matters of sixteenth-century architecture and gardens. Later in life Catherine helped promote the Saint Bartholomew's Day slaughter of the Huguenots; causality can't be proved, but stifled resentment—so many years of it!—must make its mark somewhere on the soul.

Diane's daily regimen, according to a rather prim biography I once read which was called, equivocally, *The Moon Mistress* (Diana being the goddess of the hunt, chastity, and the moon), was to rise at three in the morning, take a cold bath, and ride for three hours on horseback. Then, following a short rest, she was zestfully ready for the ardors and factions of court life. Gracefully witty accounts of these fill the pages of *The Princess of Cleves*, where, come to think of it, Madame de Lafayette also tilts towards the wife, the queen, away from the mistress. Her barbs follow a single theme. Diane is introduced "dressed in a style which would have been more suitable for ... her own granddaughter, who was just then growing up." And the princess of the title, "who was at an age when it seems impossible that any woman over twenty-five could be loved, was astonished to see the King's devotion for this grandmother."

Henry was the younger son of the great Renaissance king Francis I, and no one, not even Diane, could predict he'd end up on the throne. When fate intervened, his coronation robes, like everything else he touched, were marked with intertwined HD. Poor old multiparous Catherine.

In addition to that dawn gallop, power kept Diane young. As Madame de Lafayette puts it, she "governed the King so completely that she could be said to be mistress both of his person and of the whole realm." She built new chateaux, improved and enlarged existing ones. Her device was "Omnium victorem vici"— I conquer who conquers all. Did she mean the king? Or Time, aging and weakening lovers and the force of passion alike?

Ironically enough, Henry, who had declared his interest in Diane by wearing her colors for his first tournament at the age of twelve, died in a joust at forty. This sad event did not dim Diane's star too drastically. Catherine took back Chenonceaux and the jewels Henry had given her: a nickel revenge. The HD motifs were never erased; Diane retained her other chateaux and, more, the habit of living life beautifully. She continued, beautifully, to do as she pleased until her death.

"Which is why," I explain to my daughter as we ride down the shaded avenue leading to Chenonceaux, "I want to be Diane de Poitiers when I grow up."

I am sowing seeds, of course, preparing to reveal some of my secrets, to knife the durable balloon of conventional behavior, conventional wisdom. Diane's glorious adultery has a trickle-down effect which, I've reasoned, redeems my own adventures from shabbiness—in my own eyes and, it begins to seem possible to hope, in my daughter's eyes as well.

My desire for her approval has jelled into a curious idea. If I can submit my case to this ingenue, I will carry away significant reassurances impossible to secure by confiding in a sophisticate. Why should innocence absolve more effectively than worldliness? I don't know, but the notion is as compelling as it is irrational. And it's not just me. The men I've had relatively lengthy involvements with since being divorced have all sought signs of absolution from my children. Not one has rested easy in bed until certain the kids didn't "mind."

As we lean against the wall that overlooks Diane's Chenonceaux garden, I find in my notebook a list of the Renaissance's laws of beauty, which I read aloud:

> *three things white: skin, teeth, hands*
> *three things black: eyes, eyebrows, eyelashes*
> *three things red: lips, cheeks, nails*
> *three things long: body, hair, hands*
> *three things short: teeth, ears, feet*
> *three things narrow: mouth, waist, ankle*
> *three things big: arms, thighs, calf ...*

"Big arms and legs?" She can't believe it. We both qualify, of course, with our strong, muscular limbs, but only one of us is relaxed about it. Here's a chance to be a patient and friendly mentor in a whole new realm.

Some kids like their bodies; too many don't. My daughter has enough friends in the bizarre grip of anorexia nervosa that when she morosely complains, as she does now, "I hate my body," I feel I must challenge her.

"That stuff makes me furious. Your body works admirably for you and deserves admiration. You have no right to expect so much of it, use it so hard, and then moan and groan because you're not a dainty little sylph."

47

I go on to admit I mortified my flesh when I was her age. I thought my ass, in profile, should stick out no more than my stomach, which was flat to the point of concavity, so I wore a girdle. "Playtex. Made like a giant rubber band. Glued by sweat to the skin, which kept it in place."

"I can't imagine you in a girdle."

"Well there you are. Silliness. I got over it at college once I got serious about sports. And once some boys got serious about me, ass and all."

This mild bawdry brings on an attack of prissiness and closes down the subject. Kids become squeamish when reminded that their parents have sex lives. I should have held my tongue at sports.

Later, when we pass a band of boys lounging on their Velosolexes, she cringes at their loutish clamor as if I'd never spoken of body pride. What's more, far from perceiving me as a model worth emulating, I'm embarrassing her. When we're approaching a town, she stops to put her shirt on over her bathing suit top—so why can't I? And why do I insist on wearing that dumb hat with those dumb strings tied under my dumb chin?

Ever since our Chartres fight, my daughter has been in full command of the mapping, as she should have been all along. Her sense of direction is a marvel, and mine's so bad that I can do better by choosing the exact opposite turn from the one I think I should take, even after I've laboriously considered the position of the sun, formed a mental image of a compass, and superimposed these fleeting objectivities on the map. My daughter can't believe I made it through Italy alone, and I hardly do myself. I think the Italian system of posting a laundry list of towns accommodates my disability. Even if you stray from the right road, you're still heading for the right destination. The French system, with road markers corresponding in number and color to the lines on the map is too precise and exquisite for me.

Routing solved, food, our fuel, remains a persistent practical difficulty. In this country where the pleasures of the table are paramount, we have trouble filling our bellies.

Breakfast must be American—we can't ride thirty morning miles on croissants and coffee, so we're always seeking a *supermarché* that sells corn flakes. We eat several helpings from our multipurpose bowls, two plastic containers stenciled "Savarese Ricotta." These containers, their lids, tin cups, spoons, and our Swiss Army knives constitute our kitchen. No stove. Stoves are useless when traveling this light as there's no room to store condiments, oil, cleanup necessities. And stoves encourage abominations: dried soups that leave a chemical taste in the mouth; instant coffee. Since surpassingly good coffee is commonplace wherever we'll be, drinking instant is martyrish folly.

Lunch—bread, cheese, fruit, yogurt, and a liter of the pale sweet liquid they call *limonade*—is easy and, because breads and cheeses vary from place to place, steadily interesting. With lunch the problem is when and where to buy. Towns, on the little roads we choose, are far apart. With scant luggage space for stowing food, we must buy near where we'll eat. Food stores close for the midday break on an idiosyncratic local option basis, so we never know whether we've got time to get to the next town before the overhead doors clang resolutely down for what might as well be forever.

We've resolved to avoid restaurants until we're sick of picnics. There may still be cheap good restaurants somewhere in France, but last summer Adam and I learned to our sorrow that inflation invariably links cheap to blandly bad. So our suppers, too, are picnics, requiring us not only to buy our food before the evening closing hour but also to know, well in advance, where we'll spend the night. Nothing is more dispiriting than to roll hungry and empty-handed into a campground maddeningly perfumed with everyone else's cuisine.

We splurge on these evening picnics, adding wine, pastry, chocolate, and whatever has struck our fancy at the *charcuterie*. Nothing is as elegant as a well-stocked French deli: salade Niçoise, three or four kinds of pâté, stuffed tomatoes, stuffed mushrooms, quiches, mille-feuille-wrapped sausage, artichokes big as pineapples and cooked in something that preserves their lovely color, savory broiled chicken, ham not too much like pink flannel. All quite expensive, but the quality forgives the price and there's no tip to pay.

The single bargain still untouched by inflation is wine—light, fresh reds with no trace of rawness for under a dollar a bottle. Wine introduces a funny frustration. It tastes so good and is so cheap we want to drink lots, but because we're dehydrated we're bombed after four sips. Adam and I had the same problem, even without cycling. We'd polish off a bottle and pass out, the understanding being that whoever woke up first in the middle of the night might wake the other for conversation or dalliance.

Now when I wake under those same stars, with the same ghost of wine taste in my mouth, I don't so much miss Adam as miss that whole drama of being with a man, of sensuality. Motherhood seems to have an anaesthetizing effect. I stare at the stars and brood about why, when last year I was Mademoiselle to shopkeepers, this year I am Madame. And I brood about the institution of marriage, whose strongest justification is that children benefit from the interesting tensions generated as a man and a woman rub along together. With sex the emollient, the tensions are beneficial—so beneficial you can reverse the equation. The strongest justification for marriage, then, is ready access to sex: we two are the main event and the kids are only accidents of that event, here today, gone tomorrow. Except. Except that motherhood (even spinning along through chateau country, I'm reminded of schedules and acquisitions and the never-ending maintenance of objects, of forms) seems to have this anaesthetizing effect. Suggesting that the most plausible justification of marriage is self-canceling.

When this trip is over, my daughter will finish out the summer baby-sitting for her Cape Cod sandhills. She talks about this family incessantly. They are paragons. It sounds as if the parents enjoy and support each other as much as they enjoy and support the kids. The kids—Seth, Mouse, Clarkie—laugh and play, play and laugh. Never is heard a discouraging word. So who am I, insomniac under alien stars, to even hint to my daughter that she look elsewhere for happiness? Or reveal my dark suspicion that the justification of marriage is doomed by inherent contradictions? Ah. I've misplaced an important fact. She hasn't yet had her first white lightning kiss, isn't awake to sex, the immutable value of ready access. If she's not to marry for the wrong reasons, I must do my work well. And doubtless it's the weight and complexity of this responsibility that's dragging down the corners of my mouth, aging me into Madame.

It strikes me that she brings her family into every conversation the same way I brought in my boyfriends when I was seventeen. Earlier, noting her uncommunicativeness about Blair, I'd decided this was her way to forestall dialogue and prevent me from declaring open season on vanilla boys. But babbling about her paragons might also be a form of role play. She could be fantasizing her own well-heeled, ocean-facing future bliss. And Blair—any Blair—lacking dynamic presence, can never hope to be more than an accident of that main event.

*　　　*　　　*

We've been on the road a week. My daughter's masterly routing magically produces more downgrades than inclines. One particularly stunning performance gives us a panorama of the chateau at Amboise spread loosely along the Loire. The day is so clear we can count the antlers studding its distant towers.

I pound her back in delight. "How do you do it, time after time?"

"Pure luck."

I'm about to cry no, not luck, it's your fabulous instinct, but I shut up just in time. If luck runs out, she's not to blame, but if instinct fails, she'll assume I think she's "totally useless." I'm learning tact. Learning, I mean, that the kid should also be treated with tact, just like anyone else.

Chapter Five

I'm not sorry to be leaving the Touraine, with its memories and its tourist buses, for Burgundy. Burgundy! The name summons robust images of power and defiant independence. Looking at a somber Burgundian castle with its massive walls and arrow-slit embrasures, the chateaux of the Loire are remembered as effete. The difference in wine reflects the comparison—there's a Burgundian saying that one is hungry for wine, not thirsty.

We pass many small farms where squads of stocky women in flowered cotton shifts, absurdly tight around ass and thighs, bend awkwardly to pick strawberries. It's hard to conceive of a less functional costume—they look like an exercise class ordered to touch toes, and every last one a knee-bending cheat. We buy strawberries whenever we see them for sale, mixing them with yogurt for breakfast, *crème fraîche* for dessert, and gobbling them by handfuls in between. My daughter proclaims them her first strawberries ever, all others she's eaten having been flavored by 3000 miles of boxcar from California.

Drought here has stunted the corn and reduced streams to evil-looking trickles. Still, the land is so fully utilized and beaually tended you can't help feeling the farmers will prevail as they have for centuries. My city-bred daughter picks this up all by herself. She's also noticed that shops in the minute towns, however dusty and flyspecked, are solidly *there*—no FOR RENT signs or liquidation sales. She mentally circles this until she grasps its significance: at home, manifestations of impermanence have always distressed her, but she hadn't known, until now, that such flux is neither universal nor inevitable.

I tell her she's a clever girl and want to pick up on her idea, to compare and contrast cultures, as we used to say in the class-room, including footnotes referring to sandhill certainty cults. But I'm working on the habit of tact. Quite possibly she's been balking at my elaborations because they mean I'm "winning." We've had several reprises of our Chartres fight, and I'm begin-ning to understand why she wails, "You push too hard! You make it seem like nothing at all!"

I'm trying, now, to leave things open, to avoid pushing for every analogy. Leaving threads unknotted, squandering pedan-tic opportunities isn't easy for me, but already I've discovered that when she abruptly drops a subject it's not to snub me, but rather that a thought has struck home and she needs time to reflect and assimilate—or develop defenses against implications she finds dangerous.

We're entering a clay region, with houses built of brick instead of the creamy tufa of the river valley. There are dozens of small, old-fashioned salt-glazing potteries, tall chimneys rising from dense clutters of bowls, flowerpots, and jardinieres big as wash-tubs.

Aubigny is a sleepy town of half-timbered apricot brick houses and cottages. We have come here because there's a hostel and we're tired of *le camping*. The hostel, where we're the sole guests, is a strange place, a dirty, smelly building full of flies, built on what was once a farmyard. The dour old man and woman in charge, unlike any hostel keepers I've ever encountered, seem to be in it exclusively for the money.

We eat our supper picnic in town, in the parched, quiet garden that surrounds the sixteenth-century town hall. I decide to seize the moment, to admit it's a great relief to be away from chateau country and last summer's memories of Adam.

She stiffens protectively, then turns on me. "You're dumping him for what's-his-name. The way you dump everyone."

I'm amazed at this outburst and the blast of blame that follows. "The minute I get to know someone, out he goes. I don't even know my own father anymore. Okay. Fine. But don't ask me to meet this new guy. I never want to lay eyes on him. That way I won't mind when you dump him too."

Surreal. Left field. I'm a lost-cause addict, not a dumper. Her father had the luck to fall in love with a woman who'd marked him out, or doubtless we'd still be miserably stuck with each other. For us, any ill effects of divorce are long past; his marriage thrives, single life suits me so completely I often forget I was ever married. My daughter's reminder that ill effects persist, that she claims injury and damages, is, therefore, momentarily startling.

I collect myself and suggest that maybe the pain she feels is similar to my own. "You were helpless, acted on by your father's choices the same way I was acted on by Adam's. I didn't dump Adam. I pulled back from the hurts into a kind of limbo and John found me there."

"Well, who is he? Besides rich."

"He's not rich. He's sort of Adam's opposite. More sure of himself and what he wants out of life. Not as funny, as witty. Taller. A few years older." The next descriptive word is "married," but I can't volunteer it, for she's still my conscience, my common sense. I mumble something about John's capacity for emotional depth. "Adam can't let himself love me wholeheart-edly—partly because I'm not going to have babies at this late date. If he loves me wholeheartedly he'll have to give up his idea that a proper man has children."

This is supposed to prompt her to ask if John has children so I'll be forced to spill the rest of these troublesome beans, but again her response comes from left field. Flatly she states that Adam doesn't want children, that she's unable to imagine him with children, except for her and her brother. "*We're* his chil-dren," she insists, and I marvel at her innocence, and pity her too—for if Adam were listening he'd run for his life, fleeing her intensity and its implied burdens of commitment.

Adam would run away. Her father deserted her side to marry a stranger and live with that stranger's children. John won't leave his children to live with me.

Our parallel, unjoined lines of thought lead us into separate meditations. Tears splash. It's nice to sit in this empty, dusty French park and yield to tears, to the sepia persuasions of ten-derness and regret. I don't mean that our emotions are fake or forced, but when we've finished feeling abandoned and badly used by our men, we'll blow our noses, embrace, and feel better for the interlude. An interlude that those very men, I'd guess, would consider a moment of weakness.

Before bed the kid writes her alternate-day postcard to Blair. I have a thought. Her father is blond, so she picks boyfriends who conform to this aesthetic imprinting. Cagey, though, she also insists on a quality decidedly alien to her father—a vanilla iner-tia which obliges them to stick around until she herself hankers for a change.

But I grow Byzantine, absurd. Do other mothers labor so to sift the riddles of their daughter's juvenile affections? My resisted analogies and stifled pedantries are popping up, fully vigorous, in a new corner of the garden. The taproot's a tough one.

We awake early to a great clamor punctuated by agonized glottal screams. Hearts in our throats, we rush to the window. Not thirty feet away, in the neighboring farmyard, four men and a woman are attempting to sit on a terrified porker to hold it still for butchering. There's blood everywhere—obviously they've botched the first cut. Two children dance excitedly. The pig continues to scream. The knife flashes again, and the silence is as sudden and frightening as the screams.

Colette, that earthy Burgundian, would have raced to watch the violent gush of blood, the glazing of the eyeballs, the life twitching out of flesh. Not us.

Colette is on my mind. We're a day's ride from Saint-Sauveur-en-Puisaye, her childhood home, the "Montigny" of the Claudine stories. I've long admired her as a woman and writer, and so assigned Saint-Sauveur as our first mail drop.

To get there we climb a series of hills, the final one so steep we dismount and trudge. Described by Colette as a remote, magical preserve, complete with ivy-covered Saracen tower, Saint-Sauveur is today full of face-lifted shops selling convenience foods and plastic toys. We are reminded that, for all our exertions, we are exactly two Citroën-hours from Paris; Saint-Sauveur is *pays du weekend*.

One hotel is full, the other closed on Tuesdays. The post office is closed until morning. We decide to camp on the shores of a nearby lake which looks sizable on the map. Because this is the first time we've slept outside without the protection of a campground, we're a bit nervous, but the prospect of a swim after so many hot dry days is compensatory.

When we arrive, we count a dozen or so tents on the opposite shore where people stand fishing. We peg out our tent and change into bathing suits, but it is too shallow here and the bottom too suspect for more than a quick rinse. My amphibious daughter, who has spent every previous summer of her life inches from water, is acutely disappointed. I'd warned her at the start there'd be little swimming, and she's been stoical, but the deprivation is more drastic than she'd bargained for.

While finishing our supper in the strong, clear, orange light of the setting sun, I tell her about Colette and the sea, how she used the sea to help her raise the daughter, her only child, born to her at forty. Colette's own mother, the redoubtable Sido, had set too tireless an example of maternal perfection. Rendered inadequate by comparison, Colette sought help from the sea. To her it was a "maternal element better fitted than I to teach, ripen, and perfect the mind and body which I had merely rough-hewn."

My daughter interrupts. There's a guy spying on us. He's been staring and making kissy-smack sounds. He's just moved closer. Is much too close.

I size him up. A creep. Wormy looking. If he were more attractive he'd be more predictable—but then, in France, attractive men rarely behave this way. I put on a great show of indifference, but in truth I'm afraid to tell him to get lost, afraid to do anything that might provoke his return, in darkness, with a dark plan or with confederates. We can't even pee because he's sure to follow us into the woods. We must wait, bladders painfully tight, for the very darkness we fear.

"I keep remembering the pig."

"Well, don't. Think about getting letters tomorrow."

We're inside the tent. It is quiet and dark; we hope we've

been left alone. The thin nylon overhead bellies in a sudden breeze, and I see the knife raised to slash it open, to expose the living tissue within. Good Christ. She sleeps long before I do.

Awake at dawn, safe, I'm disgusted with myself. Invasion and violation by the foreign male! How abjectly typical. Where's all this maidenly skittishness coming from? I've never felt it before, no more than I've grown querulous over foreign plumbing or yearned for hash browns and a decent steak. Is it age? Or something to do with having a virgin in tow?

When we crawl out of the tent to discover the whole lake rimmed with decent, patient men interested solely in fish, I'm freshly ashamed.

One of the great advantages of bike touring is that you can talk to the natives easily and often, but on this trip we've had no conversations beyond utilitarian exchanges with shopkeepers. My daughter claims she's afraid to speak French. Her various teachers, obeying what must be a generic impulse, have squelched her with reports of how horribly American accents grate on tender French sensibilities. But her linguistic reluctance might also stem from maidenly skittishness. Caught from me? Infecting me? I can't decide. And maybe she's right to be wary of strangers. She's been raised in a more dangerous world than I, and hers is the world we're traveling through.

At the brand-new post office, American modular-type (brick), there are two letters for me from John. None from Adam. Even in our time of grace and belief there wouldn't have been a letter from Adam—he'd say it was too soon for him to have any news. John's letters will contain the news that he loves and misses me. What is it about this world that someone else's husband can express love more freely and frankly than a bachelor?

The kid, who's given this address to a dozen or more best friends, has no letters at all, not even from perfidious Blair. She's numb, I'm furious. How dare he! A cipher, a nothing—and guess who's going to have to pick up the pieces?

"Maybe the mails are screwed up."

"Oh, sure."

"I'm sorry, kiddo."

"What good does that do?"

"All the good I can, at the moment."

"The worst is, yours are from him."

Her venom, after our rapport in the Aubigny park, hits like a cleaver. My counterattack scorches the earth. Anyone unable to understand why children are battered and parents slain is a hypocrite or a fool.

But the ferocious moment soon passes. A fight, we've come to realize, is only a daily matter. We no longer torment ourselves with any cherished ideals of perfect accord, of absolute compatibility. We recognize ourselves as murderous and warlike: it passes. "Well for godsakes read them," she orders, not too scornfully, "get it over with so we can go."

Here is Colette on child-rearing:

> Touch what you please...enter into contact with everything around you. Touch, beneath the cat's fur, the violent movements of its little ones trying to be born. Hold the little yellow chick in your hand, and don't hurt it. You want to drink out of the beautiful Chinese cup? Drink then. But if you break it, you will be deprived, forever, of the pleasure of drinking from it. Take care: the wasp has a sting. But when all is said and done, whether you get yourself stung or not is your own affair. Knives cut, pliers pinch...Do you see? You are bleeding. Next time you'll handle it better; my advice is to try again, to touch it again...

It sounds wonderful, but she's left out the murder. *When all is said and done, whether you get yourself stung or not is your own affair.* Sorry, Colette, I can't believe you're so admirably objective. Once a woman has a child, nothing is ever again entirely her own affair. Children, as my eighty-six-year-old Boston landlady is fond of saying, are hostages to fortune. Probably a parent should dissemble, pretend children's stings are their own affair in order to persuade them that they are, ultimately, responsible for their own lives. But the lesson is too excruciating. Since we never accepted it wholly ourselves, we can't reliably teach it, so we'd better factor in the murderous feelings in hopes that they won't take us by surprise and lead to horrors, to action.

Away from Saint-Sauveur, the country is wilder. Up on a ridge, dramatic against the sky, are the crenelations of a ruined, chivalry-haunted twelfth-century castle. Entering the little town at its feet we hear something long absent from our travels—rushing water. A clean, vigorous stream courses through the town and, a bit farther on, we locate its source, the "beautiful springs" that gave the town its name, Druyes-les-Belles-Fontaines. Right at the roadside is a little church-like building in partial collapse, with a curved, half-domed apse. From the wall of the apse where an altar would be placed, water spouts, filling a sunken pool about ten by fifteen feet, and this in turn empties into the stream we passed.

Dusty, cobwebby stone benches surround this watery nave. If I were in charge, I'd make it a ceremonial place. It strongly feels like one. Men and boys some nights, women and girls others. Homage to the water genesis of our species. On Sunday, community swim and revelry.

I look up *druyes* in the dictionary: druids. Of course. But how satisfying to possess the place directly, intuitively, in advance of definitions. To escape so delightfully my pedantic habits.

What is the ideal relationship of the verbal to the purely felt or the visual? I'm reminded of my Italian trip three years ago when I met a Florentine whose pleasure it was to teach me his beloved language. He spoke no English; I'd had fifteen hours of adult education Italian. Without the purely felt, we'd never have made it.

He'd drive me out of the torpid city into the cooler mountains where we drank Chianti and enjoyed language with physical intervals. At times I *had* Italian; as if someone had slipped an auxiliary brain into my skull, I happily comprehended all he said. Excited, I'd open my mouth expecting a complex and fluent paragraph to issue forth, but of course all that came was halting baby talk. It hurt my head, this contrast—the same kind of jolt you feel when you step off a curb unawares. The root meaning of "infant" is "one unable to speak," and when you consider all the other things a baby can't do, the peculiar force of verbal frustration is more than clarified.

I love words, love knowing druids were here. What weird rituals has this place seen? I want to learn more about them—compare and contrast with Stonehenge, for instance. But even more, I love having had that recognition before the word. The rarer moment. Then why do I say "druids" to the kid? Why don't I leave her alone to feel the nonverbal vibes? I suppose it's yet another necessary discontent of civilization: we must know in order to experience the full pleasure of sometimes not knowing. The hunger that drives us beyond infancy has a stiff price—but who'd voluntarily choose otherwise?

After lunch, a pattering of rain. Refreshing. The wind is from the east. Sido used to shake her fist at the east wind, which usually brought three days of battering that wrecked her garden.

The farms here desperately need rain. Since Vézelay, our next stop, has a hostel, we could probably find it in our hearts to welcome even three wet days without too much grousing.

If I'd not already recalled my friend in Florence, steep Vézelay would provoke those memories, for with its stone walls, red tile roofs, and the surmounting basilica it looks exactly like a hill town in Tuscany. My daughter is gratifyingly enchanted when I tell her how much more of this awaits us in Italy.

For reasons still unclear to me, I haven't written my friend to alert him to our visit. When we parted, he promised to learn English, I Italian. I also promised to return *al più presto possibile*. Tears starting, he made a prediction: I would either return or have a *grand' amore*. He meant with Adam, who was having a separate vacation that summer; I'd mentioned Adam but made light of him for the duration. After a few months of sending semiliterate letters to Florence, it seemed more honest to write a kiss-off: "While you will always be in my thoughts, *caro*, today and tomorrow Adam is here with me." At this, his letters stopped and I stopped studying Italian.

It was bicycling that first brought us together. He came to my rescue in a crowded outdoor trattoria near the Duomo by signaling the waiter it was all right for me to be seated at his table. Having done that, he waited, with a circumspection unusual in Italy, for me to begin any conversation we were going to have. I soon discovered that he'd been the Italian cycling champion some ten years earlier, then had dropped out of competition to become a civil servant. He much disliked the opportunism of the *gente della corsa*, the hustling promoters.

A passionate man, but not earthy. At times even finicky, overfastidious. He had the face of one of those lounging Etruscan sarcophagus figures: big rounded jaw, high cheekbones, full cheeks into which were stitched the corners of a full mouth, cleft chin. His father had been one of Mussolini's Libyan pioneers. Born there, it amused him to call himself an African when he wasn't calling himself an Etruscan. He liked to quote Dante, repeat the lines in modern Italian, and then once more in Florentine dialect.

I was his first American friend, he claimed, and I never found any reason to disbelieve him. He was married, but lived apart from his wife. There were children, a girl and a boy.

Several times I've started to write him a postcard, but then I decide it's better to surprise him.

In Vézelay, a superb hostel, a *prix fixe* restaurant meal that efficiently disappointed every gustatory hope, and delineations of punishment for wrongdoing in the two great categories.

Venial: a pungent and freely spotted angle in the city wall bears the hand-lettered legend, *Defense d'uriner sous peine d'arrosage à jet d'eau.*

Mortal: over the main portal of the basilica, the joyous saved are being divided from the damned, whose attenuated forms are the very image of cringing shame and woe. Sins of the flesh, decidedly—long hands grope to cover wicked genitals. Wailing and lamenting, they file into the gaping jaws of a dagger-toothed crocodile. Inside the basilica, cool, crisp harmonies of gray and cream stone. The soul soars, for this is a place of balm and light. But haunted—is it not?—by the woeful damned and their fleshly reek.

What are we supposed to do with our flesh? Betimes, piss will again spatter the wall, unchastened by any cleansing jets. At home, the newest orgasm book sells briskly, and why not, since it promises redemption from the cringing shame and woe of sexual failure. Back in Chartres, the kings and queens gaze out over the endless comedy with sweet, unshaken confidence. They know something we don't, and it's not how to have multiple orgasms.

Church attendance is down, way down. The church has never effectively reconciled flesh and spirit; we're still treading that same old divided path, with the flesh currently in ascendancy.

We can't seem to tolerate differences without ascendancies. If woman is different from man, she (or he) must be less. If the spirit endures while the body turns to decay and dust, the body must be less.

The Greeks, whose gods and goddesses often lusted foolishly, whimsically, were better served, in fleshly matters, than we. But that's not the fault of Jesus, who rarely addressed the question. His statement that in heaven there is no marriage, but we are like angels with each other—that is, our communion is perfect and complete always—doesn't begin to suggest that we ought to jettison those fragments of complete communion sometimes experienced during earthly, physical, love. Nevertheless, before long, the flesh came to be devalued by the church—with the result that sins of the flesh loom large and blot out the rest, leaving war, among others, unaddressed.

I'd like to see a Hiroshima portal on a church.

Indications are that the devaluation of the flesh came into Christianity through Saint Paul, whose name was claimed by the boarding school my daughter so successfully attends. But I must resist these facile connections.

Chapter Six

Before I became a bicycle tourist, I imagined that good times rested on fair weather and reasonable terrain. In practice, these variables are secondary to a more subtle one.

True—strong headwinds persecute; rain, dreary, limits visibility and makes braking dangerous. A tight succession of roller coaster hills can be disheartening—not enough easy down to compensate for all the up. Cold stiffens and causes muscle strain, sun-blasted heat brings on headaches and desperate thirst. But for all this, the kiss of death is still the moment you start to feel your bike is no more than transportation, a relatively slow and arduous means of getting there.

Getting there derives, of course, from the automobile experience. If 300 miles a day are possible, who can rein in for thirty? Driving quite slowly, I've noticed flashes of roadside pink and wondered what kind of flower that was, but never stopped and walked back for a close look. Or something is glimpsed at the end of an avenue of trees, but it's rarely "worth" a U-turn to investigate further. U-turns are such a big deal in a car, in traffic—besides, if I keep stopping I'll never get there.

On a bike, U-turns aren't a big deal, and the best routes tempt you into making plenty of them. In fact, the most reliable antidote to those poisonous automotive speed-and-distance standards is a richly varied environment. Villages, castles, ruins, churches in generous distribution, with the threads of emerging and changing regional motifs as plot, encourage the cyclist to relish the moment at hand, to *be* there instead of focusing on destinations.

European biking is more rewarding than American, for if an American tour is tranquil, it won't be steadily leavened by architectural complexity. You must then rely on nature to hold you in the present moment, and bikes are too fast for nature. This is not to say that bikers don't enjoy birdsong, wild flowers, fresh air, vistas, but nature is best sought away from roads altogether. Hiking's the right pace for nature.

"But if you're on bicycles, you won't have time to see anything." This common objection also derives from the automobile experience, and it's false on two counts. First, the steady, regular exercise leaves you in a far more alert and receptive state than a day in a car or train. And second, if you pick your tour carefully, you are seeing and hearing things all the time—what I mean by being there.

Say you're game to try a bike tour, but have only two weeks and some stamina worries. Where should you go? An excellent choice is that part of Burgundy called the Côte d'Or. (The "gold" is the pastureland that shimmers in the autumn sun after a summer of steady nibbling by herds of sweet-faced, creamy tan cows.)

For energetic days, there are hills and a few real mountains; otherwise, a long, easy route follows the Burgundy Canal. There are stretches of wild country—wild for Europe—with forests, rock pinnacles, and hawks wheeling hungrily overhead. And multitudes of medieval castles, crumbling, unspoiled villages, ancient abbeys.

The two important cities in this region are Dijon and Beaune. Dijon is elegant and sophisticated, with Parisian ironwork along the boulevards. The old quarter, where cars are forbidden, has places to see and be seen in and art nouveau touches. Nonchalantly chic university students parade past the imposing palace of the dukes of Burgundy, dominated by the tower of Philip the Bold. What names they had, those dukes—John the Fearless, Charles the Bold. Only when such inheritors stopped being born, in the last quarter of the fifteenth century, was independent Burgundy rendered sufficiently tame to be firmly annexed by France. Next to the palace is the strangely gargoyled façade of Notre Dame, three tiers of monsters, seventeen across, furniture for a lifetime of bad dreams.

Beaune is famous for wine merchants and cellars, prettier, quieter, more intimately charming than Dijon. I wish we could have stayed in Beaune several days, if only for the wine—either unbelievably cheap or, for sampling, free.

The fifteenth-century Hôtel Dieu in Beaune is probably the best example of the odd particolored roof found in this region—severely geometric designs worked with glossy tiles, red, green, yellow, black. These roofs illustrate the way regional motifs act as plot. A minor (invisible to whizzing cars) specimen is spotted. Could be a freak. But five miles on there's another, and soon another, more elaborate this time. You're on to something. Another. Definitely on to something. Then the Hôtel Dieu draws all together in an exuberant climax. "Ah," you breathe, and "of course," for you remember that very first sign and hint—which might have been no more than a freak—of this consummate finale. You carry away not only an appreciation for the roofs, but also a most pleasant sense of your own perspicacity.

At Pouilly-en-Auxois, in a small campground on the banks of the poplar-colonnaded canal, we met an English couple on bikes who'd come down from Paris through Fontainebleau in only two days. A faster way to get to the Côte d'Or would be the train from Paris to Dijon. The French are used to bikes on trains; they hang them from hooks on special wheeled racks, as if they were sides of beef.

Even at the extremely relaxed pace of twenty or thirty miles a day, you'd see a lot of the Côte d'Or in two weeks, with ample time out for wine. What won't be seen is lots of tourists, not in the summertime. The Michelin green guide to Burgundy hasn't yet appeared in any language but French, and French tourists, as everyone knows, spend summer by the sea.

Probably because we haven't paid local taxes, it always feels like pulling a fast one to use, free, a municipal park like the one that's a short walk from the Dijon campground. A clean, sandy, and, this hot day, populous beach edges a large lake: the kid's element, at long last. She rolls and dives like a dolphin, smiling, too, like a dolphin. Underwater, her bright hair, metallic green, swirls and fans; she's rapt, at home. Unlike Colette, though, I don't enlist water as maternal backup, for when my daughter swims she's in sandhill country.

Stretching out on the sand, for her, triggers total recall of sandhill pleasures and affluence. France is forgotten. Images of adorable Mouse, sportive Seth, and baby Clarkie are as vivid as if this were merely her day off and I were visiting her on Cape Cod. Oh baby Clarkie of the marigold hair! "Clarkie's so *funny*, Mom. I'll be in the kitchen fixing lunch and all of a sudden there's this scratchy little voice, terribly serious and concerned, asking me what I'm doing. 'Making toasted cheese,' I'll say. 'That's good,' she says, 'that's good.' She practically pats me on the head—as if I'm being a good girl, you know? It's so *funny*, the way she does it—"

When kids talk about what lies close to their hearts, parents can't confess boredom any more than they can call names—or so we're instructed. We're to accept our children for what they are, misplaced enthusiasms included.

First break, I sprint for a dip.

We haven't had any separate experiences on this trip, that's the trouble. Constant contact is sucking us dry. I swim and walk and swim again, and when I return, I've been usurped by an exceedingly attractive boy and his two sidekicks. Her first foreign flirtation; she's a new woman.

I sit far enough away to leave them plenty of privacy. Mom as procuress: I hope to procure an evening alone for my own renewal. They're strangers, but that risk seems small compared to the clear and present danger of being sucked dry.

But no dice. They did indeed ask her out. She turned them down and won't say why. "Let's just drop it, okay?"

"Could you understand their French?"

"Better than they thought."

"That must've been useful."

"Yeah. The little one said he was going to ask me out but the cutie said oh no, she's for me."

"He is a cutie. Not quite your usual type."

"Oh, I don't know."

"Well, he's dark."

"Yeah. Mostly they asked about America. They feel sorry for us because we have refrigerators. They think we never get any fresh food."

"You should have gone with them."

"Well I didn't, so drop it." Next day she's morose. I'm so used to her being pissed off with me for some reason or another I don't bother to ask why, but then she wails, "I'll never see them again. I hate this part of traveling. They were so nice and

I'll never see them again, ever."

"But you'll meet more nice people. If you're open to them, they'll be open to you."

"They were so *cute*."

"So are you. And it's a big world."

I intend to comfort; she believes me callous. She's in a mood to yearn wistfully over her loss. If she'd accepted what the boys offered, she'd be on her way to accepting a disquieting truth about pleasure—it is rare, fugitive, and comes in its own time, not according to our cravings. Anyone who hopes to stand, always, on solid rock better say no and stick with the inferior, but utterly reliable, pleasure of yearning over what will never be.

The Burgundy Canal, using 189 locks to climb almost 1000 feet, connects the Yonne and Saône rivers, and still carries a moderate traffic of work and pleasure craft. We pause, outside Dijon, to watch two barges approach the same lock from different directions. Despite our confidence in French precision, we can't quite believe it's going to work.

One barge flies an American flag along with the French tricolor. "Are you American?" I ask the man at the wheel who is tanned, barefoot, bearded like Abe Lincoln. He finishes lighting his Gauloise, considers, admits it. "So are we," I say. A Gallic shrug. "Small world," he says, hoping he's finished with me.

He is. He's like one of those recently divorced women who think talking to other women at parties is a waste of time. A few years ago, he'd have tried to pass, but now he's cashing in on being American, for the French, these days, rather like us. They wear T-shirts printed OHIO STATE and CALIFORNIA COLLEGE. Denim specialty shops are either Wild West or as starred and striped as a hometown Fourth of July. Last summer Adam and I were even complimented on our efforts to speak French. This was a far cry from the frosty sixties, when all questions were repeated and answered in (bad) English—the implication being that your ears were too barbaric for any contact with their noble tongue.

While we were hitching around, Adam and I tried to check out this pro-American shift. "France will always remember American help in the war," was, in essence, the invariable response, even from young people who knew World War II only as history. My own theory is that we gained sympathy when we, too, blew it in Vietnam. Also, because of Franco-American estrangement, we stayed away for several years, German tourists taking our places. Bad as Americans are, Germans are worse.

The locks bear the date 1890, and their heavy wooden gates are hand-operated. The keepers are jolly, chatty people. Children help by yelling enthusiastically and by running to secure hawsers. Some of the keepers are middle-aged women, wearing, again, those nonfunctional, flowered shift dresses. They can't take a wide enough stance against the vigor of their cranking, and must compensate with arm muscle. The men, in contrast, can throw their whole bodies into each turn of the crank.

Canals, for me, infinitely suggest adventure, romance. Water highways. A collision of romantic river associations—across the wide Missouri, way down upon the Swanee—with the song and hopeful promise of the open road.

But no collision, just now, on the Burgundy Canal. The two barges pass, inches of free water between them and the walls of the lock. The American's is aptly called *Eel*.

We have purchased our last Michelin map, the one that, presumably, will get us to Switzerland. It is a frightening document, darkly washed with the brown ridges that signify mountains. The roads hairpinning over these ridges are marked with chevrons indicating degrees of steepness. The green, or scenic, roads have more chevrons and tighter switchbacks than any others, but my undaunted daughter resolutely traces these all the way to Geneva.

Behind us is Chalon, K-Mart modern, and the perfection, in cycling terms, of the Grosne valley: long, moderate hills, a wonderful castle at Bresse, stupendous Cluny.

In the Middle Ages, Cluny was the greatest church in Europe. Inside its ruined, vaulting, reddish-tan walls (with no sculptured sinners to distract) I profoundly feel the church's awesome power to command the souls of the faithful. Carried away is a sense of how Cluny gave significant purpose and focus to human existence. It returned, that is, as much as it took, for obviously pocketbooks were powerfully mobilized along with prayers. This feeling is not easily carried away from, say, Saint Peter's in Rome, but then Saint Peter's hasn't the poignancy of a majesty that is benign and forgivable because lying in ruins.

Behind us, too, is Carla, an American college student. Poor mild Carla, with her beautiful body and long, straight blond hair, trying to have fun touring on a new bicycle that kept presenting her with mechanical and baggage-stowing problems.

Carla is also riding to Switzerland, and in the hostel at Chalon we three pore over our maps (different publishers, same monstrous mountains). She describes her route to date. She's unerringly missed the lovely and found the ugly. Especially the human ugly. "I've been so hassled," she sighs. "I finally started wearing long pants. They're awfully hot and uncomfortable over my knees, but—" and off she fades, gently resigned.

Later she approaches me to say she'd like to team up with us as far as Geneva, for moral support and for safety.

I think, bleakly, another bike to break down, another child to test my fragile hold on adult forbearance. But could she provide diffusion and free us from the dreadful inevitability of our daily fight? "Someone your own age," I prompt, consulting privately with my daughter.

Disbelief and vigorous protest. "My age? She's not my age. Nowhere near. She's like a little baby."

Sweet Carla, thanks. When the kid compared herself to you, she decided she could let herself off the hook, and me with her. She decided she was all right, that she'd do. I hope you made out okay. I still feel like a heel for saying no, but an eternally grateful heel. Once we had the offer of your company, we stopped feeling condemned to each other's. We started having more fun. And no fights for three whole days.

Mountains. Some ranges start with roller coaster hills. The best strategy is to keep pedaling at your usual flatland cadence as you go down, even if you're racing the motor, rolling too fast for the pedaling to add any propulsion. If you coast on short hills, it's too difficult to catch the ideal moment for resumed effort, and, more important, coasting induces a psychological block against the next rise.

To climb a true mountain, you often must stand on your pedals and pull up on your handlebars, at least in the steep sections. (On the whole, I don't think mountains inflict as much pain as jogging, but then, I hate jogging.) Thirst is an incessant problem. And heat: that hot pounding in your head. The long, coasting run down—it's all right to coast with real mountains—cools heads fast. Meantime, upgrade, a wet hat helps enormously.

In some ways, mountains are easier than flats. There's usually far less wind, that element imperceptibly helpful at your back but cruelly discouraging when met head-on. (A powerful head wind forces you to hunch over the lowest part of your handlebars. You can't see much. Nor, with such a loud rushing past your ears, can you hear. The normal hazards of unrelieved introspection are further aggravated by physical stress, a combination to avoid even if you're not forty and wondering what to do with the rest of your life.) Mountains tax the neck, shoulder, and arm muscles less than flatlands. Also, while coasting, you can rise up over your handlebars and give your fork a cooling break. (I suffer, when I suffer, in the fork. My daughter suffers in the knees.)

There they are ahead, the Jura, a high blue immensity on the horizon, and ahead of them, the Alps—but we won't think about the Alps. Sufficient unto the day is the evil thereof. "Europe," I announce breezily, "was settled eons before the invention of the automobile. People managed mountains then and we can manage them now. When it's too much, we'll walk. We have lots of time."

In sad, drought-stricken Franche-Comté, after a hot, piney climb, we're overjoyed to find a cold spring running into a brimming stone tub. Having seen not a soul or a passing car for hours, we're tempted to shed our shorts and climb in. Unfortunately, the terrier in the farmhouse opposite sets up a terrific din and rouses his mistress from her midday nap. She's watching; we settle for decorous spongings.

Suddenly a car pulls up. The cops. The driver is a handsome devil who's having trouble keeping his official face in position. His partner, a very serious Adolphe Menjou, gets out and walks over to us. "Please, your papers."

He glances at our passports, surprised, in his stonefaced way, that we're Americans, and hands them to the driver, who's reached HQ on the radio. The driver begins to spell our names: mike, alpha, roger— The woman in the farmhouse (did she call the cops?) shushes her terrier.

My daughter itches to know what's up and whispers, "Is it okay to ask?" I almost burst out laughing. She's so ultra-respectful, and Menjou is so B-movie. He's been studying the long, fat earthworm of my gall bladder scar as if it were criminal evidence. She trundles out polite phrases until he understands her and answers, with chilling propriety, that this is normal procedure, absolutely normal.

HQ's obtuseness suggests otherwise. They're stuck on the kid's birthplace. "Nort' Caroleena," repeats the handsome one. "No. Car-o-lee-na. No. Charley, alpha, roger—"

Menjou again: "You are sisters? No? Truly? *Formidable.*" He shakes his head, retrieves my passport, checks for himself. "*Formidable*, Madame," he concludes, and snaps his fingers for the other passport. The driver protests. He's not quite finished. Menjou says it's all right and, touching his hat, hands us our passports. He may have clicked his heels. The driver grins openly. Both call out *bonne journée, bon voyage*, and are gone as suddenly as they came.

"Jesus," my daughter breathes, "I thought for sure we were going to end up in jail."

She's really scared. "But what on earth have we done wrong?"

Deaf ears. She knows better. Hardly a doper—not even half a drag on the group joint in order to go with the flow—she still identifies with the generation that is scooped up at borders, thrown into foreign prisons, and never heard from again.

We are in Arinthod, in the dining room of our first hotel since Versailles. Everyone is drinking Monsieur's excellent house Beaune; this and Monsieur's pleasant manner have encouraged conversation between tables. They want to talk bicycles, but I prefer politics. We haven't seen a *Herald Tribune* since Dijon and have lost track of Italian politics. Last I knew, the shock of the Moro tragedy and the revelation of scandal that forced President Leone's resignation had brought the government to a standstill. I'm concerned that the progressive left will lose ground as it always seems to at home in periods of turmoil. (For some time I've believed that the Communists could reform Italian economic and civic myopia. It is a cruel irony that the reassuringly democratic process by which these Eurocommunists hope to triumph has inflamed ultra-leftists like the Red Brigades who kidnapped and killed Aldo Moro.)

I grab the first opening. "Does Italy have a new president yet?"

Blank faces all around. I enlist my daughter's fluency to explain my interest in how the Communists are faring.

A big laugh. Oh you Americans. Always the communism. Always Italy. Poor Italy. The poor Pope. Here we concern ourselves with France. Italy—poof.

First Menjou clicking his heels, now "poof." Some days every native you meet is right out of central casting.

My daughter is much more worried about a fifties-style Red Menace than the terrorist tactics of the Red Brigades. "What if the new president is a Communist? Can we still go?"

"He won't be. But of course we'll go. The north's been Communist for years."

"Really? When you were there? And it was okay? It was? Really?"

What are they teaching her at that school? Capital—Its Enemies and Preservation? "Listen, the Italians are too fractious for monolithic menaces. There hasn't been unanimity on that peninsula since the Roman Empire. With time out for Mussolini, you understand. He did manage to bring them to a consensus of sorts for twenty years or so."

"Well yeah. What about that? How do you know communism isn't another Mussolini?"

"How do you know anything?"

"No, seriously."

"I'm perfectly serious."

"Why is the State Department afraid of communism? They must know things we don't."

"Probably. On the other hand, we're supposed to know enough to elect legislators and a president—give or take campaign promises, media packaging, and outright lies."

Oh Carla! Sacrificial lamb! We're having so much fun because of you.

Each mountain crossed has a distinct personality. Rising steeply from Arinthod are intensely green woodlands with box profuse and fragrant in the roadside sun. Glossy ivy carpets the ground under tall oaks and conifers; wildflowers run mostly in the blue-purple-pink range. We spot two enchanting ones new to us, a richly indigo columbine and a lily, clear pink, with freckled reflexive petals.

At the summit of this lush greenery we overlook the long, slim length of the Lac de Vouglans, bright camp tents dotting its shores, with the mass of the Jura beyond. The road down is carved through harsh, dry rock and is no more than a car and a half wide. We swerve madly around its abrupt switchbacks, braking constantly to stay in absolute control—we can see only fifteen or twenty feet ahead and meeting a car could be nasty. Great cresting escarpments loom overhead, signs warn of falling rocks. We're like surfers sliding under the curl at Makaha Beach.

Several times we stop to let our brake-grabbed wheels cool because someone told us superheated wheels can cause blowouts. I'm skeptical, and after a few of these halts I decide to hell with it and take the exhilarating run for all it's worth, the kid tagging more cautiously behind.

Our plan is to continue through the mountains until we get tired, and then look for a place to spend the night. It is overcast, windless. Reprieved from the sun and charged up by our plummeting descent, we're world beaters.

My daughter looks up from the map. "I bet we can make Geneva."

Make Geneva. Get there. "Not possible."

"Well, let's just see."

Just as we begin to climb the Jura, a storm breaks. Thunder cracks, reverberating through the valleys, each fresh explosion piling wildly on the echoes of the last. For a time we huddle under the eaves of a roadside shed, but it soon makes more sense to push on wet and warm than to hide here wet and cold. Climbing in rain isn't too dangerous, and, with that optimism that imbues all emergency decisions, we're positive the rain will stop for our descent.

At the gorge of Le Saut du Chien (Fried dog? I ask and get a laugh, for even language gags are allowed since Carla) the rain has eased to a drizzle. Mist rises in the sharp V of the gorge, and the surrounding mountains lie beautifully footless in retreating tones of gray. We are at 708 meters, according to the sign, and still climbing, but how much farther is anyone's guess—we've somehow lost our map and no one's around to ask in this dismal weather.

A brief downhill bit, then more climbing, down again and, abruptly, Mijoux. We're near the ski lifts of Le Manon. Mijoux has that seediness common to ski towns once the snow melts to expose the wear and tear of pursued pleasure, the cut-rate expediency of every fake chalet.

We stop to buy food but, stupidly, not to sleep. For some reason we even forget to inquire where the next town is. Only when darkness is imminent does the situation clarify. The storm and the loss of the map, which disoriented me, generated in my daughter a steely and insane determination to sleep, this night, in Geneva. Her will has been driving us like a force-twelve tail wind.

She's way ahead of me as she has been all day. I call to her to stop. She waits, impatiently. We argue. She's sure we're almost at the top. She remembers what the road looked like on the map. We can do it—once at the top it's all downhill.

"Nope. We've already gone too far. Three mountains in one day is enough. It's dangerous when you're tired."

"I'm not tired. And besides, it's dangerous to camp. What about wild animals? Where's the level ground for the tent—or are you planning to sleep out in the rain?"

She hammers away while I search for a way to penetrate the steep rocky cliff that walls the road. It seems hopeless until, with about ten minutes of daylight left, I spot something, climb up, scuffle around. "Not bad," I call down. She's frozen, defiant, balked, furious.

I'd like to belt her one, but it's a time, if ever there was, for Supermom. I drag my bike up the incline and peg out the tent. Eventually she appears, but not to help. We eat in darkness and silence, too hungry to save anything for breakfast. When we've finished, I feel vulnerable and hollow, as if I've scarcely replaced cell depletions, with no surplus for the uncertain future. Gusts of wind shake rain loose from the high firs overhead. Supermom doesn't mention renewed downpours: we're athwart a natural gully, the reason it's fairly flat here. The gully probably drains the whole mountain.

Morning dawns sunny and dry. Even our sneakers are drying. The largest beast seen was a red squirrel. My daughter is ungrateful for these miracles. Sulky and drag-ass, she has to be pried from the sack. She can't help break camp because she has to look for her barrette. She can't find her shock cords either. Her back hurts because I put the tent on top of a huge root that gouged her all night long. "Listen you—" I begin, and we have the fight I didn't dare risk last night. A million-megaton fight that shatters boulders, fells tall trees, and, with adrenaline to spare, pushes me uphill past a skull and crossbones sign— VIPÈRES—fifty feet from our camp, and uphill for five more kilometers to the summit inn where it would have been so comfy to spend the night.

On the sunlit terrace we have *tartines* and coffee and a view of La Dôle. The cups are large, Swiss style. I drink three. My daughter buys a new map and we discover we're 300 meters higher than I've climbed before on a bike.

We're almost on speaking terms when an attractive, lean, concisely muscled man on a sleek and whippy racing bike arrives from the Geneva side. Fists on hips, he shows off, executing a series of tight, symmetrical figure eights. Is he even breathing hard? He's stagey enough to pretend he's not. Soon other cyclists crest up. They're breathing hard. They're from Gex, fourteen kilometers away and 600 meters down. No race, just the morning workout of a local club. The last stragglers are panting and sweating as hard as I'd be—but then, I smugly note to myself, they carry no baggage.

"But remember, they don't have baggage," my daughter says.

"My exact thought."

She leans across the table to take my hands, giving me a long, solemn look. "Now you two girls are gonna get on your bicycles," she intones, "and cross that border into Geneva, Switzerland. Do I have it straight? And Mom? Did you see that sign with the snake warning?"

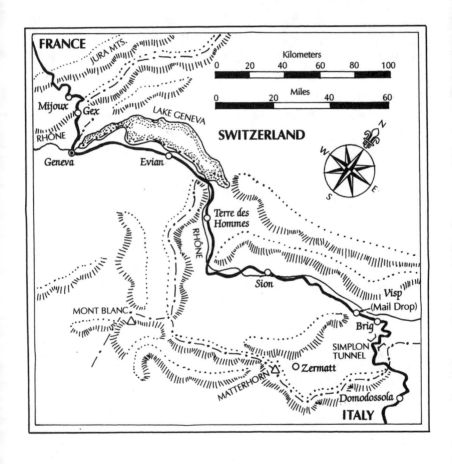

Chapter *Seven*

Geneva, after the mountains, is a glossy, prosperous shock. Since it's Switzerland, we're obliged to believe that the endless traffic, which we consider as anarchic and rude as big-city traffic anywhere, streams along according to a faultless and logical pattern, conceived by experts and fully understood by everyone but us. The reason we keep getting in trouble is not because the system is wrong but because we, intruders, lack its key. If the system were wrong, the Swiss would fix it. I have the feeling that this is only the first of many times when Swiss perfectibility will simultaneously reassure and put me on the prickly defensive.

We've been warned the hostel is a zoo, travelers piled sixteen to a room, but since hostels are supposed to promote international accord, this one, in this city, promises a confluence of starry-eyed idealism impossible to resist.

The multinational mix is there all right, but the subterranean kitchen is such a tight, inconveniently arranged squeeze and the dining room such a murky corridor that conviviality is suffocated by more urgent requirements like patience. Each hosteler stakes out an allotment of table space and sits in the gloom to down a cheapo meal—eggs, rice, Spam, sardines—as quickly as possible.

After supper we walk past Lenin's house (the plaque designates him simply "Founder of the Soviet Union") to the astonishing Rhône where large, healthy fish swim almost as visibly in the depths as the river's swan population does on its surface. Pinning down the Rhône's elusive green clarity has tormented many a phrasemaker—the journals of John Ruskin, for example, contain frequent attempts, none completely satisfying him despite his extraordinary descriptive powers.

Ruskin loved Geneva, for Mont Blanc and for geology. Lenin chafed and fretted here for a brief year, complaining of the stolid burghers. My daughter firmly sides with Ruskin, for the stunning novelty of a crystalline urban river, the promise of swimming tomorrow, and Tobler chocolate at the price of Hershey. I'm working to keep an open mind, but it's difficult. The country has been so thoroughly photographed and filmed and written about that every impression has to fight its way through a thick muffling screen of preconception.

A pair of fish hawks circle and glide, circle and glide. One makes a sudden, thrilling attack on the lucid green, but his purposeful talons remain empty. Stoop, it's called—feeble word for a movement so dramatic.

Hawks have it tough. How do they evaluate the risk of a long shot against the pain in their bellies? Obviously they can't stoop every time they spot a fish—the subsequent climb back to the required vantage takes too much strength. Do they define an acceptable range of probability? Suppose it's getting dark and they've had no luck. Will they risk energy already severely sapped on a fish outside this range? And what of the young waiting back at the nest? A terrible life, and a courageous one; still, raptors are inevitably bad guys in cartoons and Disneyflicks.

My daughter is reading a brochure aloud, and when she gets to the world peace part I realize some of my resistance to Geneva is fallout from too many newspaper headlines. The conference table. Live, deliberate diplomats here, dead and dying soldiers elsewhere. A cliché made forceful because we're right on the spot.

"Remember peace demonstrations?"

"I remember you made me go. My friends had to fight to go. Or sneak."

The era of demonstrations preceded that of Adam and the various indulgences he secured me. Different from other mothers, I was then primarily weird, potentially embarrassing.

"Did your friends wish they had peacenik mamas too?"

"I guess so. But not if they knew the truth."

"Which was?"

"At home you threw steaming hot oatmeal right at my head."

Like hawks, children have it tough. "Poor Furley." It's her baby name, gathering up the nicest furry kitten and little girl associations. Hugged, she smiles forgivingly. Murderous as our battles now rage, she knows I'm glad she's grown too big to smack or fling more oatmeal at.

It takes forever for sixteen women to settle in for the night. We have, besides, a snorer. Another sixteen, with their own compulsions to drop heavy objects, giggle, snap on overhead lights, and rustle through belongings, are separated by a thin partition that quits five feet from the ceiling.

In the early hours, sleep is further disrupted by a delegation of larking males. Next morning in the women's bathroom, international understanding is greatly advanced as we compare notes, snicker, and shake our heads in the way that universally summarizes feminine response to masculine roguery.

"Another tranquil night in Peace City?" I offer the kid, but the Alpine fever is upon her. Soon we're spinning along the southern shore of Lake Geneva, parklike and curiously militaristic. Manicured battalions of roses, lances—the masts of moored sailboats—thickly grouped beyond, rigging going chink-a-chink in the fresh morning breeze.

We stop at a consciously antique inn for breakfast, but as we approach the porch where people are eating at two long tables, a tiny old woman rises up to scold: *"Non! Non! Fermé. Fermé."* A young woman calms her and invites us to join them. It's a center for the elderly and small children, recreation and day care. Clever Swiss, giving the oldsters the grandparental option—or, less sentimentally, neatly disposing of the two most unabashedly self-absorbed age groups under a single roof.

Fresh hot bread, steaming milk, chocolate, coffee, and homemade strawberry jam are set before us. The rest of the staff has gathered; we are going to be utilized as a diversion. Fine, but because of that self-absorption, only the staff is diverted. My daughter manages the French while I busily stuff myself. When we finish, I ask if we can pay something, and the young woman in charge shakes her head. *"Vous êtes trop de bonne heure, Madame"*—I'm "too early"—not yet old enough.

A customs barrier. We're briefly back in France, pedaling along the shoreline to Chemins Jussy, where the public beach is overrun by school children of ten or eleven having a class outing. The star attraction is a fleet of molded plastic kayaks, built to take the collisions of childish water wars. The kids waiting for a chance at the kayaks are playing a tame version of drop the handkerchief with their matronly teacher. The only person who has any fun is the dropper. Turns, therefore, are lengthy, but the game, which would quickly provoke rebellion and defection on a Boston playground, induces here only increasingly languid obedience. A dropee, when finally chosen, responds with torpid befuddlement. Several boys too lively for this nonsense wear canteens slung over their shoulders and pursue ardent filling rituals at the water spigot. These are magic, bottomless canteens. We never see them emptied, only filled.

My daughter sighs and leans against me. "Wish you were a little kid again?" I ask, and get what I'm looking for—her Furley smile, which happily concedes any soft spots she feels good about having.

Although clean, the pebbled beach is not particularly pleasant. Later we discover that after Evian we can stop anywhere and claim a private stretch of rock and water for our own.

Elegant Evian is full of carved, spruce flower beds set in velvety grass, of ancients on promenade, of big new Mercedeses. The baths—*les thermes*—are housed in a large, fanciful rotunda. I'm tempted to take the plunge but the kid's adamant. They'll be too expensive. And there's something sinister about them, some taint of the massage parlor.

Yes. The genteel languor of Evian has an unmistakable speckling of naughtiness, of Edwardian decadence. At this point, an elderly man, Belgian, Edwardian as we could order, comes to begin a conversation. When we tell him we stay often at *les campings*, he shakes a warning finger. "Watch out for the boys, especially in Italy." My daughter giggles. The Belgian thinks it's because she's boy-crazy, but I know better. She's seen the targets of campground passion—*la toilette, la cuisine, le blanchissage*: women, soapsuds to their elbows, bending over their scrubbing-boards as alertly submissive as Pompeians making love. We promise we'll be very careful.

I decide that when I'm the Belgian's age I'll come back with John for an Edwardian revel—make Evian our base for botanical expeditions in the mountains. Loosen up our stringy old muscles at *les thermes* in between hikes—brambles, as Nabokov called them in *Ada*. Botanical rambles. Nabokov. I can see from here Montreux, where he lived out his last years. For a man who stayed married to the same woman all his long life, he knew unerringly and intricately the lineaments of forbidden and frustrated love.

When John and I are seventy, his wife and Adam will be in their mid-sixties—Adam too callow, still, for Evian, John's wife still too virginal. We'll leave them home together: it would be a kindness.

My favorite Edwardian romance is that of a bachelor whose childhood sweetheart loved him from afar until she was a virgin of seventy and he a resilient roué of seventy-four. He then married her, a bare month after he'd had to make the sad but unavoidable decision to put his mistress of thirty years standing in a nursing home.

Another true story I like less well is of a man who loved a married woman for twenty years. He gave himself up utterly to her, abandoning his brilliant youthful promise as a scholar, his hopes of a home and family. He believed he had met love's most severe test when he honestly felt he no longer minded what he had lost or missed, when celebration of what actually was yielded a radiance that left no room for dark resentments and brooding over what might have been. Then, with absolutely no warning, she died. Two years later, he's still climbing out of the wreckage. Sees a shrink every day.

Issues of getting there and being there are not confined to cycle tours. Getting there, the end of the movie, is marriage. No one would dream of asking the bride in the first story if she minded losing her old, free life of ideal love unimpeded by fleshy, smelly reality. The second story seemingly illustrates a triumph over the desire for conventional destinations, conventional resolutions—except for the wild card of death. Then why the wreck-age, why the necessity of heavy, long-term shrinking? Being there is supposed to supply its own reward. As in cycling.

Well, but for all our determination to "be there" all the time, we do have our destination, Rome. Subtract Rome and we lose the whole shape of this experience. Take away orgasm and there goes the shape of lovemaking. Possibly this man cherished an unhelpful or mistaken Rome.

What I want to know more about is the different destinations available to a couple, the Romes that will shape my life with Adam, or with John, or whomever. Marriage won't do. I have no confidence in marriage. There simply has to be a better Rome than marriage, though it appears more elusive of definition than the precise nature of the Rhône's color as it flows swiftly out of Geneva.

When planning this trip I must have asked a dozen globetrotters to describe Switzerland's Rhône valley. No one was able to do so in terms useful to me. This, then, is the truth: pancake-flat, with the Alps abrupt at both edges. Lots of traffic, but tolerable. The stringent Swiss standards for noise and emissions help. We aren't gassed or deafened by trucks as on a major highway in, say, Italy. Road shoulders are broad and smoothly paved.

Heavily industrialized, the valley is sometimes beautiful, with marvels of agriculture engineering in the terraced and irrigated vineyards. Oddly, there are more vineyards here than we saw in Burgundy, though the wine, Neuchâtel, isn't in the league by far. The river, so preternaturally clear at the other end of Lake Geneva, is limestone-clouded, cold, and much too rambunctious, in late June, for swimming.

A good map shows any number of small roads looping up from the highway, paralleling it through several little towns, and then turning back down. We are too impatient for our mail drop at Visp, for our Alpine crossing, for Italy; we ploddingly stick with the highway.

Along the shoulders of the mountains are campgrounds, but, lazy, we appropriate a pasture for the night. It's insufficiently secluded for any country but mannerly Switzerland; although a tiny hand-lettered sign tells us we are near a village called Terre des Hommes, we think only in terms of trespass, not of carnal invasion. Switzerland is the apotheosis of sandhill. We wash in a clear, icy irrigation ditch and plunder a neglected cherry tree. The night is quiet and dawn rosy, luminous, full of bluebells and cowbells.

Sion has architecture, the medieval fortresses of Valère and Tourbillon, each perched high on its own defensible pinnacle. Other tourists are climbing up for a look around, but not us. We're not here for the architecture, we're just in transit, heading with all speed possible for either an ignominious tunneling train ride or a heroic ordeal, it's not yet decided.

Around two in the afternoon the heat wins and we pull over. Half-asleep in a patch of shade, we're startled by a shouting man. He tells us he's looking for his dog, a boxer. "You understand boxer? Good, good."

He wears brown anklets and sandals and an extremely skimpy pair of shorts hoisted high over his round little tummy. It occurs to me I've yet to see a sexy Swiss, man or woman. The sandhill factor? The winters freeze it out of them?

He wants a chat. German would be his choice, but we must make do with mixed French and English. "Has much changed now that women can vote?" I ask.

He considers my question very American, very droll. "The ladies are not interested in politics. In the last local election, only twelve percent voted."

"Even so. A progressive country like Switzerland waiting that long to give a basic right to half its population—I'm amazed."

He laughs, shrugs. "The ladies are concerned with the home."

Les expositions de meubles, my daughter offers, to show agreement. She's been horrified by the huge highway stores full of elaborately tasteless furniture that are here even more shockingly out of scale than in France, where we first noticed them.

Her reference is, perhaps, too obscure for him. He returns to the subject of his dog. "The dog disappears often. He is— He has—"

"Wanderlust?" I suggest. He loves this. He's been groping toward a complex idea, and the cliché in my language turns out to be the *mot juste* of his. His estimation of us is revised upward; we're more cultivated than he presumed.

He grows animated. "Excuse, please, but why do you ride such bicycles?"

"Why not?"

He taps the dropped, racing handlebars. "These are not right for you. They are for men."

"The other kind aren't so good for riding."

"But women do not have such bicycles as these. I must tell you, when I first saw you, I thought you were boys." He laughs. "Yes! It's true! Boys."

That does it. I've had enough of him, his little tummy, and his convictions. The kid waxes righteous. "In Geneva we saw girls with bikes like ours." (We counted two.)

Jovially setting her straight: "No, I think not. Not in Geneva."

"Excuse, please," I say, "but we must now resume our nap. I hope you find your dog."

"Oh, the dog is like a woman. He will return when he is hungry."

When he's out of earshot, my daughter explodes. "What a *creep*."

"A creep," I agree, and, because I'm hoping to expand her view of the world, I deny myself the relief of yielding to the soothing contradictions of prejudice. At root, that man is a kraut: his fatal flaw.

A friend of mine, admittedly a Jew, argues that prejudice against Germans has to be a contradiction in terms, because, by definition, prejudice is irrational.

Last summer Adam and I had a startling encounter with a German couple in Amboise. In their mid-thirties, they were the absolute antithesis of the rich, loud, terrifying Germans we'd met thus far, and were traveling with their two very sweet young children in a small caravan. They invited us inside to join them for wine. It was like the cabin of a well-designed boat, a place for everything, everything in place. The husband, Peter, was studying for an advanced degree in sociology. He planned to work with prisoners, in prison reform.

A gentle, soft-spoken man, obviously loved and respected by his wife and kids. Still, an electric spark flew around the table and his mouth grew stiff and tight when he told us he'd left a career in the army—the career of his father before him—to enter this new field. Adam and I, as one always does, politely ignored the whole touchy subject; if pressed, we'd disallow the probability of Peter's father, or any other German of his acquaintance, having fought anywhere but on the Eastern front. Against them, that is, not us.

Later, talking politics, we moved through inflation and social unrest to the student demonstrations of the sixties. Then—zap!—more electricity. We'd arrived at Vietnam. And these gentle, kindly Germans were being evasively polite about *our* war.

I've recalled that moment whenever my daughter and I encounter the touring German young—giants of both sexes, legs furred densely with gold, money/document cases hung around their necks like religious medals. And I've summoned Bach and Beethoven and Marlene Dietrich. Still, I bet I won't find the time to visit Germany, not for years and years.

We've entered German-speaking Switzerland, neither of us having a particle of the language. For once, then, we don't have to make the effort, give it a try. We can howl with irresponsible laughter over every absurdly polysyllabic road sign. An interval of carefree infancy before the onerous burden of communicating with the natives passes from my daughter to me.

Visp is welcomed as our second mail drop. Alpine jitters have made us keenly hungry for the comfort of letters and we hit the post office immediately. My daughter, dreading a reprise of Saint-Sauveur, holds her breath until the pile is sorted. It's okay: one from Blair (received grudgingly—too little too late?), two from girls, and one from "a friend who's a boy, not a boyfriend. I wish you'd quit that."

Quit attempting to fray Blair's primacy, she means. I haven't been subtle—though, surprisingly, my innuendoes have caused no ructions. Is this good? Or further demonstration that Blair is merely one of a series, more where he came from? And is *that* good?

I have one letter from my father, one from Adam, and four from John. On objective counts, Adam's is the most interesting, packed with the exploits and foibles of our common friends. John can only reiterate that he loves me, misses me: there's nothing so hermetic as illicit love. My father, who prefers the past, briefly reviews an undergraduate trip to Europe. He writes the letter of a man who swears his sleep has not once been stirred by dream or nightmare.

"At least he writes." Hers, she means, "never" does. Oh Daddies! The first men in our lives, model and standard for all who follow. No wonder the going gets rough.

We stop at the station to check out the Simplon Tunnel. Bicycles are allowed, it's not expensive, train departures are frequent.

All right then. For prep, one of your standard tourist-trap day trips—train to Zermatt, to the good life, the ultraviolet meridional Alpine bioclimate. After a Saturday of wandering on foot, of flowery meadows, wine, pastries, and soulful contemplations of the Matterhorn, we'll wake up early Sunday morning ready to confront our destiny.

As it develops, Zermatt makes our decision easy and inescapable.

The midget red train from Visp takes just over an hour. Initially, we are stirred by glimpses of gorges and snowcapped peaks, but travel lethargy soon sets in and our eyelids droop. A cyclist, a racer, toils upgrade on the road adjacent. He can't, of course, keep up with the train, much as its passengers lean out the windows to shout encouragement. I suppose they think he's exhausting himself, which is funny because my train-worn daughter has fallen asleep, and only duty to the increasingly spectacular scenery is keeping me awake.

The trails directly above the village of Zermatt that work toward the Matterhorn are laid out for pleasant walking. We climb and picnic and watch the mountain for several hours. It is sometimes hung with clouds, sometimes standing clear in high-contrast vividness. A sociable place, Zermatt. On the trails people say *grüss Gott* and we entertain drop-in company throughout our long picnic, including a backpacker from Muncie, Indiana.

Someone nearby is shooting—target practice—and everyone has a lot to say about it: "They ban cars from the town and then allow this crass, this inappropriate, this din—gunshot in Switzerland, so *wrong*—"

Doing the village, we pass and repass the same faces. The shops are pricey and elegant. Bored, we buy the *Herald Tribune* and settle into a pricey and elegant café. The kid orders a two-dollar extravaganza made of coffee, cream, ice cream, and whipped cream, studded with fragile, crisp vanilla cookies. Eating seems to be the major diversion here—I'm expecting, any moment, to go into sugar shock.

We're so habituated to taking off whenever we've had enough that the train schedule seems an outrageous usurpation of personal freedom. The sun's down; it's cold; there's nothing to do. The good restaurants won't open for another hour, so we settle for an après ski rathskeller that could be in Vermont—the same beery fried meat smell, the same rock music. And even the same customers, only more so: a dozen high-school kids from Jacksonville, Florida, sent by their trusting parents to something called The Swiss Experience. Hiking, rock climbing, white water, survival, skiing. For some, their very first snow.

This group, clearly, is the goof-off contingent. Chain-smoking, they compare the swellings, shin splints, bruises, and Ace bandages that excuse them from having, this day, an Experience.

Two boys enter magisterially. "Oh no," the cry rises, "not again, you guys—" They order schnapps and beer. It's a nightly ritual; they're favorites of the gang. The schnapps is tossed down, the beer chugalugged, a watery-eyed "Pah!" from both of them, and another round ordered. "Oh you *guys*— You guys are out of your *minds*."

The chic and savvy waitress serves the second round, stands back, and applauds when the deed is done.

Two loose, dreamy grins on the heroes. The fans wait breathlessly, then one hero observes to the other, "We're late." They stand up, teeter, stabilize, leave.

I am nonplused, thunderstruck. Talk about grace under fire! The urbanity of the brat! Seconds away from having the top of his head fly off, from passing out cold, from blowing lunch—I visualize the projectile vomit of a colicky newborn—or all three at once, this child has the wit and presence to announce, urbanely, "We're late." He and his associate have given us the performance of our day, but: "We're late"—other audiences await them, they must, so sorry, leave us. The implied social affluence is staggering.

An envious silence settles. "Those guys are crazy," a girl bursts out, but none of us can get it up enough to support her or even nod in agreement. We've been wiped out.

On the train ride back down, my daughter rebounds and won't let go. "What a joke. What a bunch of phonies. I can just see them home in Florida telling their parents how tough it was. The Swiss Experience. What a laugh."

It is only a tiny leap from this to tomorrow, to our own Experience. No question now, we must attempt the classic event, the real thing. Something definitive, monumental, must be inserted between their teenagerhood and her own in order to erase all suspicion of common ground. A simmering little kettle of fastidious disdain, the only way I'd get her on that tunnel train would be bound and gagged.

And I'm right with her. Heroism is infectious. If that child, at that moment, could say, "We're late," I can certainly ride a bicycle over the Alps.

Chapter Eight

At seven-thirty we are in Brig, so flat a greased marble wouldn't roll down Main Street. By seven-forty I'm thoroughly winded and seriously questioning whether I can continue—the transition from valley floor to mountain range is this abrupt.

Spotting the turnoff for the pass, my daughter yells, "I'm psyched," and tears off in a sprint, hare to my tortoise, though, as far as I'm concerned, without the competitive currents working on that fabled pair. Mothers of my vintage usually don't have a lot of ego invested in strength and athletic prowess. The physical qualities we admire tend to be aesthetic rather than purely operative. Obvious drawbacks aside, this bias as least spares us the nuisance emotions of competitiveness that blight many a father-son adventure.

And if, for her part, the kid feels subversively triumphant, she's hiding it well. I labor around the bend of a switchback and there she stands, cool and easy, waiting for me to catch up. The instant I see her my will to persevere at the pedals drains away. I want desperately to dismount and walk the remaining distance—an impulse to fight because only a drag would dismount and walk, and I don't want to be a drag. She is patient, solicitous. "Are you all right? You're not going to have a heart attack, are you?" She hasn't, of course, the foggiest notion of a heart attack, except that adults have them. What she means is, you're not too old for this, are you?—though she probably doesn't have a clear idea of "too old" either. Who does? Back in the Jura, I now realize, I could have softened her disappointment by trotting out the ironclad excuse that I was too old to race to Geneva, but it never occurred to me. When I hit a psychological bottom is when I feel too old, not when I'm simply physically stressed.

One tremendous consolation is that the highway is beautifully engineered, with ample shoulders and continuous steel safety barriers. I spot, far below, a small old-fashioned farm—thick, irregular stone slabs roofing the low sunburnt wooden buildings—and crash right into the safety barrier. Some kind of optical disorientation. It will be necessary to dismount for lingering examinations of the scenery.

Because it is Sunday, we are spared trucks, and people in the few cars out early on this glorious day call cheerful encouragements. Some even pay the supreme compliment of the smiling, silent wave. My daughter wishes for the fiftieth time that we had American flags on our panniers, "just to show them."

The mountain is a monster soda fountain of streaming fresh cold water for splashing and wetting hats and drinking. Visibility is excellent and the ever-expanding panorama of snowcapped peaks makes me glad for poets. Byron, for one:

> ... *Above me are the Alps,*
> *The palaces of Nature, whose vast walls*
> *Have pinnacled in clouds their snowy scalps*
> *And throned Eternity in icy halls*
> *Of cold sublimity, where forms and falls*
> *The avalanche—the thunderbolt of snow!*

We take the spiritual and recreational clout of the Alps for granted, but according to an English authority, Sir Gavin de Beer, for centuries these mountains were feared and hated obstacles. His book, *Early Travellers in the Alps*, describes the primitive conditions that prevailed. No place for a lady, though in 1532 the Swiss scholar Thomas Platter crossed the Grimsel Pass (our own second choice) with his wife. The month was October; the unlucky woman's clothes froze to her body. (Platter's boyhood, spent as a goatherd in the high Alpine pastures, may have accounted for a degree of carelessness.) John Evelyn, whose diary is a mine of insights into seventeenth-century life, crossed the Simplon in 1646 and loathed every minute of it, from the "horrid and fearful crags" to the "wretched and infamous" lodgings.

More mellow, Sir Gavin notes, was the reaction of Joseph Addison, a leading wit of London's eighteenth-century coffeehouse period. The Alps, he wrote, "fill the mind with an agreeable kind of horror." Still, it was left to the Romantics to teach us high altitude rapture.

Wordsworth climbed the Simplon for the first time in 1790, traveling light—a few possessions tied up in a bandanna. When he reached the top he "grieved" because it was over. I envision him scaling the heights, head thrown back, sleeves ballooning, wind raking his hair, hoping it would never end. More poets followed Wordsworth's lead—Byron, of course, one of them—and painters, tourists, and the great waves of Victorian climbers, peak after peak falling to their determined assaults. Men, then women, proved that "inaccessible" was merely a state of mind. And today, with funiculars skeining everywhere and these smooth, if steep, highways, my daughter and I presume to consider ourselves embarked on a heroic ordeal.

In our case, the state of mind that, but for Zermatt, would

have put us aboard the tunnel train, better safe than sorry, is a trick of technology, which once again has limited rather than, as advertised, expanded our choices. Not only has the automobile made cycling dangerous, it has also defined norms of physical capability. Without even owning a car, I'm persuaded that it is normal to drive and that everything else is beyond the norm, "inaccessible," a test, an ordeal.

I take a snapshot of my daughter at the snow line. She looks mightily pleased with herself. Her shoulders are back, her stance has the poised alertness I've seen her assume on the squash court. Match point: the Swiss Experience Floridians are about to be annihilated. Then she photographs me. I know how I'll look. My heels will seem to be sinking into the concrete pavement, as if it were soft tar. The picture will illustrate not only trepidation but also the ill effects of gravity's having pulled me down for forty years. I try to straighten up and can't. No sensation in legs or feet. I must be hung on a pair of meat hooks set beneath my shoulder blades, and if my heels weren't mired in gravity, I'd flap like a union suit on a washline. This physical test, more severe than I've yet attempted, has attenuated, spent, canceled my flesh. Will, not muscle and sinew, pumps these pedals around and laboriously around.

"Why are we doing this? To say we have, or to prove we can?"

Climb, rest, climb again. The physical dimension is strictly mechanical, my bicycle a will-propelled machine. At one point in the crank's rotation there's a hesitation that requires an extra force of will. (Not muscle.) A flash: the clock on the wall, sixth-grade arithmetic class, monitoring the minutes of that ordeal in jumps of five. Bodilessly slumped in my hard wooden desk seat, I am pure will. It is five minutes and counting to the hour of release. I do not wait passively; I focus, concentrate, drive the hand of that clock past its maddening hesitation. My act of will obliges it to move.

The kid continues kind and patient, the road's a marvel. Well-lighted short tunnels and roofed, wide-swinging snow galleries tame some of the steepness, and yes, I realize I'm praising technology. I admit it freely. Cyclists should enjoy the very best roads human ingenuity can devise, and have them all to themselves.

Rest. Climb. She's ahead. By the time I catch up, she'll be ready to press on. I'll be ready to die.

"You okay?" she calls.

"Yeah. You?"

"Me? Sure."

"I mean, want to go on? You don't have to wait for me."

"Don't worry, I need the rest too."

Her tact, if I still had a body, would bring tears to my eyes.

Suddenly the road is level. It is the summit. We did it. Made it.

And feel what? Relief? Triumph? We grin and shout and pummel each other, pretending. Why are we such frauds? Why don't we grieve like Wordsworth? I clown for the camera, striking a cruciform pose at the summit marker: 2005 meters, way over our previous Jura record of 1325. I've pasted on a prideful smirk, but I'm bereft. We've done it. And? So? What will take the place of the rich, dense distractions of ordeal? Or, paradoxically, the simplicity of ordeal? The sense of loss, of void, at this altitude, leaves me gasping.

Action is called for. We shuffle over to the souvenir shop-cum-restaurant to buy, after absurd debate, the postcards on which we'll perpetuate our fraudulence in writing. "Three cheers for us! And womankind! The well-earned view has a special sweetness!!!"

Time to go. Too absent-mindedly for safety, we saddle up and roll, rather than ride, down to Italy.

*   *   *

It's lucky we didn't attempt to bike up the south face, because these galleries and tunnels are poorly lit or pitch-black, and the risky, disorienting gloom is far easier to survive downgrade. Here, too, are Evelyn's horrid rocky crags, enormous quelling heaves of snowcapped rock directly on top of us instead of off in the romantic distance as before. Once below the snow line, great cataracts of water accentuate rather than relieve the stark aridity of this strange lunar region. Wordsworth's lines on the Simplon call it a "hollow rent" full of "winds thwarting winds bewildered and forlorn" and "rocks that muttered." Dark and dangerous images dominate. He has to work hard to join them to the joyous confirmation he sought in Nature. Familiar as I am with this poetic evidence, the savage landscape continues to surprise, probably because I think of the south, toward Italy, as more tame and civilized than the north, toward Switzerland.

"Civilized!" my daughter squeaks. She can't get over an incident at the customs barrier, where a traffic tie-up inspired a swarthy young Italian wearing an audacious bikini to release his two German shepherds from his car. The dogs, confused by the immediately resumed traffic, dodged crazily around, barking frantically. Much honking, multilingual yelling, and slamming on of brakes, including ours—the terrified dogs, hurtling blindly, would have knocked us flat. Their owner, laughing merrily, left his Fiat in midstream, both doors wide open, engine running, to take off after his pets, shouting with impartial good will at them and anything else with ears. Except for us and the dogs, everyone had a wonderful time, even the Swiss customs officials.

Down and down we go, following the Diveria River to the Toce, hoping there will be no more climbing, because we're at the limits of our strength. As always when it's coasting time, I'm ahead, faster than my daughter, faster than a car would dare. I concentrate on the road surface, repeatedly checking the front wheel and its quick-release hub, the slender metal assembly that keeps disaster at bay. If it let go, I'd see a momentary wobble and then, unless I automatically tucked like a somersaulting diver, that's all I'd see for a good long time.

Four o'clock, sun hot and high, we're still wearing nylon jackets to cut the chill of our own wind. As the valley broadens, it is more carelessly treated. Proliferating factories surrounded by heaped refuse, roadsides strewn freely with garbage, often offensively domestic in origin, packed into neat aquamarine or white plastic sacks. Though one could confidently eat off the floors of the houses that generated this mess, Italian standards of cleanliness are strikingly inconsistent. Chuck your trash anywhere, but lick a postage stamp and the clerk who sold it to you will go into shock.

"Can we get out of here?"

"Fast as possible. What say—Maggiore? Treat ourselves to a hotel room?"

"And a swim?"

A few miles beyond Domodossola, three boys on motorcycles pass me to close in on my daughter, one tailgating, one flanking, and one pulling in front so abruptly that she skids and falls. Miraculously, the tailgater narrowly misses plowing right over her. I'm about thirty feet behind, but catch up like a shot and scream my head off. They scatter, and I attempt to comfort my poor child, my fine brave girl who just crossed the Alps, brought down by these miserable louts—I can't bear it.

They have circled and are back with us, expressions of theatrical contrition on their unlovely adolescent faces. I wish I could wade into them, take them apart, wipe up the road with them, but all I can do is scream furiously until they give up and leave us forever.

When she calms a bit, when I'm sure nothing but her spirit—her spirit!—is broken, we decide to pack it in for the day, save the lake and swimming for tomorrow.

The nearest hotel is a meager little curbside place in a town devoid of attraction, but, fortunately, the *padrone* is the kind of Italian who makes travel in this country memorable for women, especially single women. That is, he projects infinite personal interest tempered by infinitely polite restraint, and you understand he is not motivated by, say, your pretty eyes or good legs, but simply because you are a woman.

My daughter, too shell-shocked to trust the perfection of his restraint, casts a cold eye until the good dinner he serves us, and the good wine, do their work.

Shortly afterward, we crawl gratefully into our clean, thriftily darned sheets. Before we sleep, I thank her for the day. "I'd never have chanced it without you, you know. Unforgettable—the best present you could possibly give me."

She is pleased and for a moment I see her again as she was on the ascent, strong and poised and happy. But she's had a bad afternoon. "Mom? Why do they do it, those men? They look so dumb, hanging out of their little cars, waving their arms at you—they look like some weird giant bug."

"*Bella! Bella!*" I groan, imitating.

"But if they want to get something going with you, why do they act so dumb?"

"It's just their funny way." I don't want to clamp a ridiculing lid on the phenomenon of Italian male behavior too fast. I hope she can loosen up enough, in a few days, to enjoy playing back to these dudes. The game is fun when you're in the mood, and can be ignored otherwise. Besides, sensing sexual power in the abstract leads to interesting self-confrontations impossible to come by in demure Boston. Wasn't I thinking, in part, of precisely this when I decided Italy would put some wind in the kid's sails? Wasn't I visualizing the elaborately beseeching Italian men who would playfully tease her out of her distressing sandhill prissiness?

Certainly their yearning and beseeching did as much for me, my first visit, as Bernini's fountains. It was the Dark Ages. The women's movement had not yet surfaced to help me understand I was more than an insufficient, weak boy of some sort. That frank, noisy, abstract appreciation of my womanliness gave me an endorsing jolt I badly needed.

None of this is sorted out enough to discuss with a mistrustful and sleepy daughter. I do add, however, that when I was here before I never ran into anything I couldn't handle, and I was alone. "The main thing is that those boys aren't typical. Much more typical is the *padrone*. And as I said way back in Boston, it's a given. Italian men feel culturally impelled to behave as if they're prostrated by adoration for every passing woman. Their styles range from comic to subtle, but the game's the same. You can play too. You don't have to, but you can—and you can choose your own rules. But don't go assuming people are out to hurt you. Those boys didn't intend to hurt you. It was carelessness."

"Did that nut at customs want to hurt his dogs?"

"More carelessness."

Silence, then: "I was thinking about Carla. We should have let her come with us, the poor kid."

We devour double breakfasts, boggling the *padrone*, and thoughtfully study our first Italian map. Once centimeter to five kilometers, it was designed for cars and is too crude for the kid's taste. "I can't work with this thing," she sniffs, but I suspect hedging. The lakes are my turf, whether I have any sense of direction or not, and she's understandably diffident about asserting herself against a veteran. To help out, I observe that we were so fixated on the Alps we never got around to Italy. "I mean, now that we're here, where should we go? The northern parts of the lakes are supposed to be the most beautiful."

"Yeah, but there's just this one shore road. We'll be asking for it with traffic. And look at these tunnels. Why would they be lighted if the ones on the Simplon highway weren't?"

Her point's a good one; we won't risk the shore roads. I vote for the *traghetto* across the waists of the long lakes, Maggiore and Como, with tours around the little lakes, Lugano and Iseo.

"Isn't that cheating, to take a ferry?"

"Is a bridge cheating?"

"No."

"Then neither is a ferry."

"Hey. Lugano's in Switzerland." The apotheosis of sandhill never looked better to her and, after the louts, who could blame her? But she'll love Italy before long, as everyone must.

We ride past great villas with the square towers and painted wall designs characteristic of the region. Many have been converted to hotels, though not with invariable success. The failures, their guests stolen by campgrounds, are crumbling, abandoned hulks with gardens overgrown and choked by weeds. I am well ahead of my daughter and lost in melancholy musings about elegance reduced to dust and weeds when I hear her screaming.

I double back to find her locked in a struggle with a man on a motor scooter. He hears me before he sees me and releases her. As he passes me, he wags a wet and brazenly mocking tongue. He doesn't care if I see his face—I'm helpless and can do nothing against him.

"You told me it wouldn't happen again and I believed you

and it was *worse*," she sobs. The story is unspeakable: he matched his pace to hers and grabbed her crotch. She almost fell. He just grabbed tighter and laughed. She beat on his arm with all her might and he just kept squeezing and laughing. "He got his thumb right *in* me, Mom." We limp to the *traghetto*. I'm completely at a loss, unable to offer any help beyond pretending optimism I don't feel. Is it going to be like this for three weeks? Was my ability to handle incidents that came my way during previous visits to Italy only a factor of age and experience? Maybe those women who angrily reject all sexual gaming as disguised hostility are right, and the rest of this trip will reveal just how vicious the players can be.

What should I do? Brought to this country to become more receptive, my daughter has drawn completely into herself. She sticks to my side like a limpet, trembling when she has to move independently enough to stow her bike on the ferry. As we leave the shore, I keep an arm around her and talk hard. "This is a tourist area. People are far from home, free to behave badly with no neighbors watching. We'll leave the lakes as fast as we can. Meantime, look across there—it's lovely."

And it is, surpassingly lovely, distance erasing every barbarism. Dark verticals of cypress frame each ochre or sienna villa, mountains rise steeply from the lake. A world of blue: water, mountains, sky. Not for her, though. Her hot forehead is pressed against my shoulder; she's sealed tight, impervious. No one's going to catch her off guard again, ever.

A bearded German tourist approaches to talk bicycles. She shivers, breaking my heart, but at the same time I'm scared of her banked and baffled rage. She's clinging to me not because I can mend her but because I'm all she has left. I must be vigilant—one blunder and she'll dump the whole vile chamber pot on my head.

I apply more sociology: "The north is loaded with industrial workers who have migrated from the *mezzogiorno*, the south. Southerners can't behave in this relatively free environment. They're used to the restrictions and habits of their villages, especially in regard to women."

"How do you know he was from the south?"

"By looking at him. Short and dark, right? Northerners are tall and quite fair."

Ah. She believes. We've got ourselves a workable scapegoat. A reprehensible solace, but this is an emergency. "Actually," I continue, "that idea comes from my friend in Florence, the bicycling champion, remember? Florentines call Italy Garibaldi's Mistake because he unified it, brought in the south."

"So what?"

"So once we get away from here we'll be okay. Bergamo, Verona—no big industry there. And Venice is great. You'll love Venice."

"Then what're we doing here in the first place?"

Too peevish. She's pushing, ready to dump it on me. Should I remind her she'd been pestering to swim? Or borrow from Colette: The men are your problem, not mine, and anger with me won't solve anything. Learn to cope with them or not—it's really your own affair.

Impossible. "Because this is where you end up if you take the best bicycle route over the Alps," is what I neutrally produce.

Off the ferry, heading north before we cut over to Lugano, we're tagged by two young men on motorcycles. "Allo? Allo? *Sprechen Sie Deutsch? Parlez-vous français?*"

I'm riding shotgun, so I'm close by to shout, "Go away, get lost." The kid's trembling so hard she has to stop, me with her.

They circle back: "Allo? *Sprechen Sie Deutsch?*"

"Listen," I advise her, "they're friendlies, I'm sure of it. They just want to talk for a while, then they'll leave and we can continue. I'm going to speak to them, okay?"

She can't stop crying. "Every time I hear one of those motors all I can think of is that guy—"

We've attracted attention. A car pulls over, then another. The motorcyclists disappear, fun spoiled by too much company. A whole Italian family bustles out of the first car, the father carrying in one hand a glass and in the other a bottle of wine. "For the Fräulein," he urges, pouring generously. His wife chatters too rapidly for me to catch more than indignation and the repeated phrase *brutti ragazzi*. The driver of the second car, short, dark, "southern," so sincerely and liquidly troubled that I may giggle, offers to accompany us wherever we want to go. He and his Fiat, at our service—he'll be our *cavaliere*.

When a third car stops, my daughter knows that the only escape is to compose herself. "But what if they're up ahead, lurking?"

"I said, I think they're friendlies. But want this man to come with us?"

"No! I want to be alone. Can you get rid of them all?"

I wonder. The family thinks the *cavaliere* has a great idea. His selfless thrust into the breach has excited even the *bambini*. We sip more wine. I tell them we're not German but American, inadvertently causing the Samaritan flames to burn hotter and brighter. "No, *grazie, signora, signori*, no. *Grazie*, but it pleases us to be alone. *Grazie*. No."

At length, convinced, they drive off in search of other errands of mercy, leaving us to achieve Lugano without further incident.

After shabby, potholed Italy, Swiss Lugano seems solidly affluent, with pretty parks, elegant piazzas, and expensive shops lining cool arcades. We waste valuable swimming time searching for the Italian Touring Club, which supposedly sells large-scale maps. When the office is located, we learn they don't have them and don't know who does. Italians, my daughter wrathfully fumes, are too stupid to have decent maps. Italy, I begin to fully understand, is "mine," and misadventure will be my fault. The air will be thick with flung gauntlets no true adult would stoop to pick up—though I might, through blundering, or if she pushes me too hard. She's allowed leeway because of the *brutti;* she has all my concern and sympathy. But she must not take advantage. If she starts needling me simply to relieve ordinary travel stress, I, with my own anxieties, may well collect a gauntlet or two. Difficulty in obtaining maps comes under the heading of ordinary travel stress.

"Ease off a bit," I warn, and she throws me a look of complete, if malevolent, comprehension. The *brutti* have disrupted our old ground rules and boundaries—but that doesn't mean I won't frame new ones.

The campground, at the northern tip of the lake, is full, but the woman in charge will allow us to stay one night since we have no car. We hit the beach the minute the sun, having aggravated our tempers throughout the afternoon, sinks behind the western rim of mountains.

Our fellow campers, uniformly Dutch, give our exiguous camping rig the usual hilarious appraisal. Several young towheads express themselves by chucking pebbles at us while we swim.

A teenage girl visits. She is sixteen and speaks careful classroom English. From Rotterdam. This is her twelfth summer here. "Many return each summer. We enjoy to go dancing at the *cantina*. When small, I enjoyed to go to the amusement park.

My father enjoys to play tennis." (The campground has two clay courts, something I've not encountered before.)

She is very shy and nice. I have the feeling someone, possibly one of her four brothers, dared her to scout us. We tell her parts of our story, but when she leaves, my daughter is dismissive: "Imagine being dragged here year after year. Twelve years of those toilets."

They are admittedly foul, but, on the heels of that shy European politeness, her richbitch American tone grates. "What if you had a lot of kids and not much money and wanted a vacation in the sun?"

A light, disdainful laugh. "I don't ever intend to be in that position."

Let it pass, let it pass. Snobbery is rooted in fear, and she's right to fear twelve years of those toilets. I wish she could recognize the equally nasty traps and lures of wealth, but this is no time to teach her. Should've done that when she was young and pliant. Before she'd mastered the sandhill doctrine that snobbery is synonymous with discernment. And certainly before experiments with my doctrines had saturated her day with indelible horrors.

Checking out, I have a word with the manager. "*I brutti*—what can we do? How can we frighten them away?"

She shakes her head. "You have a beautiful daughter, very beautiful. It is to be expected."

She is, herself, good-looking enough to have attracted plenty of unwanted attention, and doubtless she'll have to endure plenty more before they'll let her rest. We exchange, she and I, a pleasant, wordless commiseration, which helps me far more than her skeptically offered suggestion that I shout for the police.

"She says you are a beautiful girl, very beautiful."

"Is that all?"

"We should yell for the police."

"Huh."

"The thing is, you're doomed by your beauty."

She's confused. In her world, good looks are a protection. The more you have, the more respectfully people treat you. She's turned this around and decided, on her own, that if these men and boys treat her disrespectfully, carelessly, it implies they consider her nothing. No more than a dog to terrify at whim.

"Bella ragazza," I tease gently, *"molto bella."*

She's getting it, a little. She feels better. I hug her tight, privately swearing that from here on I will hold in my mind the image of her happy sprint up the Simplon, not her snobbish shortcomings.

Chapter *Nine*

The metaphysical niceties of being instead of getting there have been shelved. Our intention is to ride every day as fast and far as possible until we've escaped the lakes region. After Lugano comes Como, legendary Como. My expectations are pessimistic: more confrontations with *i brutti*, more ruined, melancholy villas, and, I've been warned, polluted water.

Three years ago, in Ravenna, I met a vacationing industrialist from Como. Paolo, a tall, plump man about my own age, remembered an Italy of unpaved roads, of disgraceful absence of progress. Still a bachelor, he lived with his war widow mother right on the lake. The city of Como, he told me, is small, but has advantages. After work, for example, he could hop into his motorboat and go for a spin. "And swimming too?" I asked. "No. The lake is too dirty there for swimming." I went on and on about the tragedy of this until he interrupted. "*Senti.* You Americans can afford to talk about pollution. You have everything. Let us have everything too. Then we will sit down with you and discuss pollution."

Near the *traghetto* dock is a tourist attraction I had singled out before rude reality necessitated a change of itinerary, the gardens of the Villa Carlotta. My daughter, bribed by a colossal Toblerone bar, will permit a brief stopover.

Italian gardens! While visits to cathedrals and museums are, for me, inescapably shadowed by duty, gardens are pure pleasure, and these sublimely match my hopes.

They are built in three, sometimes four, tiers rising from only a few hundred feet of lakefront. Through sorceries of layout, this relatively small area gives an impression of measureless space—the space of Versailles, oppositely achieved, oppositely felt.

Terraced paths lead from one surprise to another, in a rhythm that densely but exquisitely accommodates human appetites for rest, suspense, and revelation. At the precise dramatic moment, we happen upon a diminutive mossy grotto, a quiet pool, a spirited fountain. Our favorite fountain was a composition of swaggering and grotesque dwarves, spitting brattily, daring us to mind. Always there are fresh vistas of the lake with steep, perfect Bellagio on the opposite shore—bright red-roofed houses tucked into the dark and abrupt mountainside.

The villa, an overrestored second fiddle, divides the garden. One side is all moist and ferny and deciduous dapplings and lizards quick in the fallen leaves. The other side is dry, with uncounted varieties of cactus, an intricate rock garden, beds of furiously blooming annuals, high, thick azalea hedges, and specimen evergreens, including a giant sequoia captured in California as a seedling. Orchids and staghorn ferns in peaty baskets hang from some of the taller tree trunks. And then, just as we begin to wonder what could possibly serve as a finale, we step out onto a little viewing platform that overlooks a glade of palmetto canopied by tall beech trees. Through some trick of perspective, this artful glade has no termination. Its green infinity is

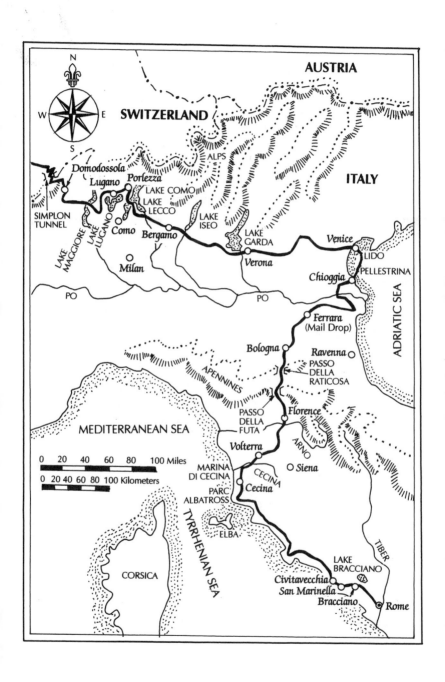

access to primeval jungle, to Rima the Bird Girl. I can almost hear her song.

On the map, Lago di Como looks like a prancing majorette holding her baton overhead. The back, or east, leg of the majorette is called Lago di Lecco. As a result of riding along that lake on the Feast of Saints Peter and Paul, a half-holiday, I know how the world will end. Not with Death on a Pale Horse, plagues of locusts, rains of brimstone mixed with blood and all that elaborate Biblical *mise en scène*, but simply with everyone, Third World, everyone, bikini-clad, driving something, probably a Cadillac, to the beach. The planet will disappear in a terminal shudder of chemical affront and aesthetic despair.

A goofy elation sets in when you and your quiet, unobtrusive bike are pitted against this level of merrymaking. Between the traffic-choked road and the body-clogged Lecco is a strip of beaten and abused earth perhaps fifteen feet wide. This is devoted to eating, sunning, shrieking, and the sportive revving of engines. As the frenzy intensifies, I feel mad laughter burbling up—scary, hysterical, gallows laughter, the kind that ends in uncontrollable tears, so better not start, not with at least ten more no-exit miles to endure.

With troubles of my own, I don't attend to my daughter more than to ride shotgun as usual (we pass unmolested except verbally, substantiating the idea that when friends and neighbors are watching, people behave; these are family groups, assembly line co-workers), and not until we're away from the lake do I learn that the poor kid has not been aware it's a holiday. Numbly resigned, she's been assuming this nightmare is standard Italian procedure—that we're in for three more weeks of just precisely this.

"But my God. You know I love Italy, and how in the world

could I love that?"

"You love lots of weird things. You loved—" and she ticks off a short but deadly list of social experiments. Oh ho. The fleshly celebrations of the Italians; my fleshly celebrations of the bedroom. Give flesh and inch and you open the floodgates to horrors. One careless inch and "weird things" will seize you by your enthralled throat and have their ghastly way with you.

Pushing it, in stupefying heat, we reach Bergamo. I ask a gloriously handsome traffic cop directions to the hostel, but between my geographical dyslexia and possible errors in translation, we're flying blind. Soon doubt obliges us to consult another man, again handsome, who speaks English and is also pushing his baby in a stroller. This evidence of *machismo* under control enhances his credibility, so when he insists the hostel is in Alta Città, miles from where we are in Bassa, we believe him. Our U-turn brings us to another cop who uses the fatal phrase, *sempre diritto*. Whenever an Italian says straight ahead, it's a sure sign that he or she is unsure, but (a national trait) would rather die than admit it.

We pedal halfheartedly straight ahead until a toothless old *nonno*, identifying our quest by our packs and foreign appearance, flags us down. The hostel, he informs us, is right up there on that hill, but not yet ready. Under construction, in fact.

A car stops: three young people, a father, and a mother. They review our case with the *nonno* and decide we should seek lodging at Villa Santa Maria. "A convent?" I ask. No, not a convent. A quiet place, clean and cheap. Follow them.

It is a large, new building of American parochial-school yellow brick. We wait in the silent, shadowy lobby for someone to come and deal with us. One of the young men speaks a little English, and even though I've briefed the family in Italian—I am her mother; Paris to Rome *sempre biciclette*—they are too amazed to accept the information until he translates it back to me in English and I confirm yes, that's right, Paris to Rome, yes, my daughter. (The lobby's mirror testifies that I look as I feel, my age and then some. That they can't believe I'm the mother absolutely demonstrates the propagandistic impact of packaging.)

A sour-faced woman in black appears and we're sidelined during a lengthy discussion, not about rooms and sleeping, but the more compelling, to Italians, issue of food. Sourpuss can't feed us. It takes her several hundred words to explain why: with the holiday, she has insufficient bread. We must go to a pizza place.

I try to persuade sourpuss that we'll abstain from bread, but she either can't understand my Italian or regards the concept of a breadless meal as too outlandish for credence. "Pizza," she repeats, "pizza."

The family won't hear of it. We are invited to Rosaria's house, nearby, for dinner. First a shower and a little rest, and then Rosaria will return for us.

We have, apparently, the whole top floor of the villa to ourselves, including a luxurious double bath at the end of the hall with torrents of hot water for shampoos and mutual back scrubs. We stretch out on our immaculate sheets. I fight the impulse to cover my nakedness—there's no lock on the door.

"A happy ending," I say.

"Oh boy. Here it comes. This is the Italy you remember, right?"

"Matter of fact, yes. The Italians are just like you. When they're good, they're very very good, and when they're bad, they're horrid."

"How do you know this isn't a setup for something horrid?"

"Of course. You've noticed the doors have no locks. In the dead of the night they'll creep in here and we'll be trussed up and delivered to New Guinea for missionary stew."

"No, seriously, what is this place?"

"A sanatorium for mad monks who've committed unspeakable acts upon young girls. And boys."

I read, she dozes off. She is a graceful sleeper, one small, tapered hand laid gracefully in the palm of the other, her cheek endearingly at rest against them. Her eyelids are a tender violet. *Bella ragazza.* My heart will burst, so fierce is my tenderness, my determination to protect.

Rosaria's spacious apartment, in a complex of modern three-story buildings, is full of objects and surfaces that catch even the gentle evening light. The expensive-looking furniture has an aggressive, machined patina; its taut damask upholstery will never fade, spot, or sag. We retreat to the roomy kitchen—color-coordinated (avocado) dishwasher, stove, wall oven, refrigerator-freezer—as American as our hostess in her dungaree skirt and T-shirt.

She is petite, rather childish, twenty-two, a student at the University of Milan, and engaged to marry Eduardo in three months. We met him before, in the car with his brother Marco and their parents. Her parents (this is their home) will arrive shortly.

Lots of nervous laughter accompanies this information. Rosaria may be having second thoughts about her generous impulse towards us. And why not? She speaks no English; my Italian works imperfectly. We're too foreign. She's never in her whole life met a divorced person. (This blurted, she's painfully worried she has offended me.) And how is she to contend with the nimbus of stiff unease radiating from my silent daughter? For that matter, how am I to? What ails the kid? If I don't watch out, she'll grab from me with both hands, take all I have, and scheme or wail for more—then, turnabout, be completely undone by the offerings of a stranger.

On the table is an impressive array of goodies—salami, fontina cheese, sliced tuna smothered in hollandaise sauce, tomatoes confettied with fresh basil, mineral water cold from the refrigerator. (After weeks of tepid to cool drinks, this alone makes a feast.) But does a divorced foreigner eat such things? Does her child? Who can be certain? Rosaria flutters her hands helplessly. "Pantomime enthusiasm and appetite, okay?" I hiss tersely, which wins me a baleful look followed by wooden compliance. The three of us know exactly how we're supposed to act—we've seen this movie hundreds of times—but we keep muffing lines, missing cues, flubbing business. We can't quite pull it off.

My daughter hunches into her chair as if determined to use not even space. The less she takes, the more I overcompensate, and the more recklessly Rosaria offers. "Wine? You wish wine? Good. I will get it from the *cantina*."

Thinking this means a corner grocery and an opportunity for me to treat, I grab my wallet and follow her.

The *cantina* turns out to be their basement storage room. There must be a thousand bottles of homemade wine here, stored on their sides, along with the last word in skis, bright molded ski boots, and fishing gear. "You wish white? Red?" My intended treat, aborted, has brought her new botheration. She hasn't a clue which bottle to choose, for young women do not know such things, even if they're about to be married.

Back upstairs, while urging us to eat, she stops short. "What should I call you? Oh no, not your first name, I couldn't—you are a mama, a signora. A signora on a bicycle. It is very difficult."

The doorbell. Reinforcements at last. Eduardo and Marco. Marco is a medical student at Bologna and speaks some English.

Eduardo I recognize instantly: sandhill. On their heels come Rosaria's mother and father, everyone talking at once. Mama criticizes everything her daughter has done. That is not enough food. We must eat something hot. Macaroni? An omelet? We protest: this is fine, this is what we like, but she starts rattling around at sink and stove anyway. Rosaria rolls her eyes meaningfully at Eduardo, but no one can stay mad at Mama.

Mama's a pisser. Bright blue eyes that don't miss a trick. She tells us she'd love to ride a bicycle but, at fifty, her legs are too old. Out stretches an exceedingly shapely leg for us to admire. Papa leans from his chair to pay her calf thorough, caressing homage. At these senile antics, Rosaria buries her face in Eduardo's neck. Next Papa interrogates us. He's flirtatious, full of innuendo. He's aware that he's bugging his daughter and means to. What's it to him if she scowls and hides her face?

Mama sets steaming plates of spaghetti alla carbonara in front of us and indicates a large bowlful of grated cheese. Our sprinklings are too delicate to suit her, so she dumps on a proper amount. My daughter giggles happily. Mama's a pro; we're safe in her hands. With Mama around, a kid can relax, eat unscrutinized, watch the movie instead of having to act in it.

At least, some kids can relax. Rosaria, offended by Papa, usurped by Mama, looks wan, petulant.

To nudge her back into stage center, I ask if she'll continue her studies after marriage. A frisson. This has not yet been decided. Eduardo is committed to his work here in the bank. He did not go to the university. And since the university at Bergamo does not have a mathematics faculty (astonishingly, she's a math major), it is "very difficult."

As Marco laboriously pins down details of my academic and work history, Rosaria alternately cuddles Eduardo (proving she forgives his lack of higher education) and studies me. Is she calculating the cause and effect of free ways and divorce/failure? Or is she wondering how I get away with it? "You are," she repeats approvingly, "a very young mother." I wish I had enough language and that the two of us could escape for a long talk together. Maybe she, too, longs to get away with it instead of hitching up to Eduardo the sandhill. I could give her the advice my own daughter so impatiently brushes aside.

Clearly, Rosaria disregards her own mother's lead, missing the message that Mama is also "young," perhaps because Mama's youth isn't for freedom and the open road but only to make Papa act like a disgusting old goat.

Okay. For the sake of discussion, say both daughters marry for the wrong reason. Which is worse off—mine who can "easily" divorce, or the one who can't, but has society and tradition helping her to grin and bear it?

Insoluble. Mama's the one I should annex for a long talk. She could tell me how to be a pro, how to provide safe hands. And share with me the secret that floats her, gaily self-assured, above the bog of a prudish, skittish daughter on the verge of a marriage that seems, even to my interloping eyes, problematic.

What Rosaria and Eduardo reliably have in common, it soon emerges, is religion. When the talk turns to this subject, Papa takes ostentatious leave of us. They are Christians, followers of the spirit of Christ. Catholic, but not in the established mode where, they feel, the form dominates the spirit. They're aware that in the United States are many Christians; they regard Jimmy Carter favorably. Some American Mormons visited Bergamo and stayed with Marco and Eduardo for three days. "A sect," Rosaria sniffs. "They spoke very good Italian," Marco reproves her, but agrees that Catholicism, despite its errors, has an ancient and indisputable validity.

"Are there many Christians like you in Italy?"

"Several hundred only. It is a very new movement."

Their group has recently held a proselytizing fair. Folk dancing, folk singers, handicrafts—everything simple, traditional. They are excited about the good that may derive from the Mariapolis, a conference of priests and laymen being held right now. Many of the priests are staying at Villa Santa Maria.

When I translate for my daughter she blushes, reminded of the mad and wicked monks.

Giovanna, a friend, drops in. Rosaria presents us with proprietary flourish, but Giovanna couldn't care less. Nor does she care to discuss the Mariapolis. She's bought three new bathing suits. One she doesn't like. Will Rosaria accept it as a gift? She begins to describe it at length. Rosaria wants to listen, but she's torn because Marco is still holding forth on spiritual matters, and Marco's approval is crucial to her even though it's his younger, lesser brother she's marrying.

After supper we drive to Alta Città, the old city, crowded with people seeking a breath of air this hot, still evening. Eduardo buys us ice cream at a famous stand. "Wonderful," I lie; it's ordinary. My daughter shoots me a look that's comically skeptical. I've given Italian ice cream an enormous buildup, but because of Marco's unpredictable comprehension of English, I can't level with her in front of him. Instead, by way of establishing standards, I mention Tre Scalini in Rome, Vivoli in Florence. Embarrassed, they confess they've never stepped foot in either city, "although we hope to visit America soon." My translation compounds the kid's disbelief. We're going by bike and they haven't even hopped on a train?

I write out our address, promising to introduce them to our best ice cream as well as some Boston friends, Pentecostal Catholics. "They speak Italian—and, like you, often bring foreigners home for a meal. Like you they act in the spirit of Christ."

The tribute is sincere enough but sounds fake in my ears. My face aches from polite smiling, and the strain of thinking in two languages has gotten to me. Around us lies the lovely old city, with St. Mark's lion everywhere—Bergamo once belonged to Venice. We are having a rare treat, an insider's look, but I can't really feel the place the way I could if my daughter and I were alone.

"Had enough?" I whisper to her.

She has. Doubtless our hosts have had enough of us hours ago, but they are too sweetly and generously at our disposal to say so. Why are good, kind people invariably dull? For all my smiling, I haven't really laughed since we left Mama and Papa. I can't wait to ask the kid if she noticed how Rosaria was bugged by her parents' frank and earthy ways.

"Oh you. You're so critical."

Her mildest rebuke. What she says when I censure sandhills that she herself has reservations about. She remembers that abyss of awkwardness and discomfort Mama saved us from.

"How far is it from Bergamo to Rome?"

"Three-four hundred miles."

"And Florence is even closer. Unbelievable. What did they say about the political situation?"

"Not much. Still no president. Mostly they're involved with the Kingdom of Heaven."

"So do we worry about strikes and stuff or not?"

"Demonstrations, riots, terrorism, and kidnapping? Not, I gather, in Bergamo."

"No, really."

"Remember the Frenchman who said, 'Italy, poof'? It's like that here, except they say, 'the rest of Italy, poof.'"

"Unbelievable."

"Sectional."

*   *   *

In the morning the priests watch us strap on our luggage. *Forza* is the operative word for us. Soft and well-fed, these men remind me of American priests I've met—the same heartiness and determination to seem a good joe. "You should address the Mariapolis," one suggests. It's a joke, but I like his association of physical strength—*forza*—with moral authority. Reminds me of old New England, of home folks training for the Boston Marathon.

At breakfast, later, my daughter says, "I could kill you for talking about them creeping into our room. I had dreams about it all night long."

"Me too." But wait—it wasn't a dream. Someone did come in. A priest, someone, opened the door and stood silhouetted in the hall light. I woke up enough to tell him he had the wrong room. He didn't go away. No, I said as loudly and firmly as possible, no. Then he closed the door and went away. A curious episode, but of no more significance than a dream, less disruptive than those larking boys in Geneva. My secret to keep, I decide—why blight Bergamo's happy ending?

Every shopkeeper so feelingly sighs, *"Caldo, no?"* that we become convinced the heat is freakish and therefore short-lived. Here today, gone before we tackle the hill country in the tomorrows ahead. Meantime, we are at Lago d'Iseo: swim break.

The shore is walled off into profiteering preserves. We choose a likely one and pay seventy-five cents "for everything—lockers, picnic tables, everything." Too late we learn that to get to water deep enough for swimming we must rent a pedalboat at two dollars an hour. I react strongly to this banditry because at this very lake I once swam in deep, clear water not ten feet from my tent; like all returning travelers, I want the only changes to be improvements. My daughter, dying for a swim, normally a fluent spender of my cash, hangs back, suffering a paralyzing attack of frugality. We enlist the lifeguard in our dithers. He agrees the boats are a ripoff but can't do more for us than repeat his advice: don't try wading to deep water, it's 500 meters of guck. At length, more to break the tiresome stalemate of indecision than anything else, I buy an hour of *Anitra*—"Duck."

Out in *Anitra*, bobbing along on her yellow and red plastic pontoons, leaning luxuriously back against her comfortable seats, performing in unison the stroke that conquered the Simplon, we are overcome by giggles. We love it. We're having the time of our lives. And the source of our dithering hesitation is fully revealed: throughout this trip, we've scornfully derided pedalboats and other extruded lumpeneuropean toys—but here we sit, having the time of our lives. It is bliss, relaxing in our chairs, tumbling off into the lovely clear water whenever we feel like it. Sail and speedboats, proper boats, pass us by without comment, another plus—we're proles, beneath notice. I am so giddy from sunlight and hilarity that I dive in with my only, my utterly essential, glasses on and grab them just before they slide into the depths.

We have never laughed together like this, my daughter and I, never with such abandon. She steers both the boat and the continuing joke of the boat. There's no limit to her inspiration. She is a *brutto ragazzo* astride his giant motorcycle. Pedaling furiously, she imitates the sexual growls of gear changes. "Allo?" she mimics seductively. *"Parlez-vous français?"* I have to beg her to stop or I'll be too weak to swim.

In the aftermath, she offers this: "You know Twinkies? How terrible they are with that greasy sweet filling? And how every so often you've just got to have one? Well, I think pedalboats are like Twinkies."

"To sneak or to flaunt?"

She ponders it. "Both at once? Does that make sense?"

I am absolutely delighted with her. And later, when we encounter yet another squadron of *brutti*, she stands up to them. "Get lost or I'll call the cops. I'll kick your teeth in. I'll bust your nose and knees."

It works; she prevails. Our mocking and laughing interlude has put steel in her spine, authority in her voice. Has she remembered Adam's farewell advice about yelling in your own language? I won't ask. This is our moment, our victory. Shoulder to shoulder! Amazon sisterhood!

That night, more magical accord—we both begin to menstruate.

Chapter Ten

We are collapsed in a café at the shaded end of the Piazza dei Signori in Verona. It is too hot to move, to breathe. Out in the square all is bleached, reduced, two-dimensional. The sentinel row of statues, the *signori*, stand like cardboard cutouts against a pale and fainting sky.

"These hot days is the mad blood stirring"—at a nearby table, a fat, red-faced man in a tight fawn-colored suit has been buying for a slim, young, decorative trio, two women and a man. They are foreigners, either German or Dutch. The table, loaded with bottles and glasses, shows they've made a serious and expensive effort to beat the heat with booze. Too expensive: the red-faced man believes himself cheated. Rising to his feet, he crumples up the bill and throws it in the waiter's face. He pounds the table, making the bottles dance. The young man tries to intervene and is brushed away by a bearish swipe of the fawn-colored arm. More angry words, then a second swipe of that thick arm. The waiter expertly ducks and comes up swinging. The red-faced man backs into the loaded table, which topples with a rich, glassy crash. The women scream. Other café personnel rush to separate the combatants. The police arrive. The red-faced man, yelling and struggling, is led away. The women sob noisily into the breast of the young man. The waiter is reassured and justified by his colleagues.

"Mercutio," my daughter breathes appreciatively. She's seen Zeffirelli's *Romeo and Juliet* three times and remembers how this square, filled with white dust and flat white light, beautifully demonstrated the reductions and erasures of Mercutio's madness.

Romeo and Juliet. Verona's star attraction. I don't, nowadays, feel properly sad about them. I can't, as the phrase goes, relate to teenage tragedy. I crave stories about aging star-crossed lovers, lovers who retain their courage and faith and romantic intensity even as they lose earning capacity, hair, muscle tone, and teeth. Teeth. I probe with my tongue the tooth that needs root canal work. It has three roots, possibly four, each to be slowly, painfully, expensively reamed. Today it's acting up. Why didn't I take care of it before I left home? For the pleasure of playing Russian roulette with the arcana of foreign dentistry? Besides, even if I cheat the odds, where, following the multiple exhaustions of this trip, will I find the money and fortitude for my dentist at home?

Existentially speaking, Montague and Capulet feuds are chicken feed compared to pending root canal work.

What really happens in *Romeo and Juliet*? Two rich, beautiful, popular kids fall in love and soon after die. They not only know exactly what they want from each other, they know exactly—and blamelessly—why it is forbidden them. No jiltings, no faintheartedness, no oedipal pitfalls along the path of their love.

Most love stories, especially in the movies, end with a wedding. Marriage signifies a happy ending. In *Romeo and Juliet* the

129

wedding is pro forma, the ending tragic.

But look what this pair missed. They never had to learn that love demands more than momentary will and courage, more than the isolated, daring, dramatic act. Although they did discover that happiness hangs from a thread fearfully fragile and slender, they were spared the more terrible knowledge that this thread stubbornly, tormentingly, resists final rupture. That we are born suckers who remain suckers, tormented by the hope and lure of happiness until the end—an end not in our own hands, not of our own choosing.

Obstacles confound all lovers. Romeo and Juliet, beauty and love undimmed, took on exactly one obstacle. Lovers who are no longer teenagers must endure an infinity of them, some quotidian and boring, others startling and terrifying. Give me, then, stories of endurance, love undimmed by the ravages of endurance. Tales of lovers who doggedly and courageously devise yet another patched, leaky compromise, hoping they can scull it through the worst of the winter. I want to sit at their feet, learn their strategies, these lovers disqualified by age, experience, and skepticism from marriage or suicide—from the solutions of movies, of teenagers.

The campground at Verona is called, of course, *Romeo e Giulietta*. My daughter disappears for a long time, returning with the good news that she's been studying Italian Touring Club maps with a Dutch couple, also cyclists, and that we can buy our own "T.C.I.'s"—she tosses it off like the cartographic authority she is—at a bookstore near the coliseum. (This structure, Roman, huge, intact, is used for operatic extravaganzas, but it can't compete with "Juliet's Balcony." Indeed, it seems intrusive in a town one is accustomed to regarding as English and Elizabethan.)

I go to talk with the kid's new friends, two people utterly in love with Italy. Impossible to praise it enough. At the deliberately easy pace of thirty miles a day, they crossed the border at the Riviera and at once struck out for the level countryside, keeping always a safe distance from smoggy Turin and Milan. This is the first night they've had to resort to a campground; before, they were the wined and dined guests of farm families, sleeping in fields or barns or, often as not, in the farmer's own bed, at his insistence. "They are a wonderfully friendly people, the Italians— they are so happy to have us bicycling here, enjoying their country in a simple way."

They are impressed by our Alpine crossing but, themselves, would never go anywhere near the lakes. "Dreadful places, full of ignorant Dutch tourists whose idea of travel is to gossip with the same people day after day."

Measured against this cheerful enthusiasm, our complaints of *i brutti* seem querulous whines. I slink away feeling jealous and gypped—they've done so much more with their opportunity than we have. My daughter, however, is confident: once we get decent maps, we'll do as well as they. "*Speriamo,*" I say dolefully, my self-reliance riddled by bad tooth, jealousy, and the knowledge that this Dutch woman rides protected by her robust male companion.

Though I don't explain my mood, my daughter leans over from her sleeping bag to give me a long hug.

"Poor Mummy, she can't break down. She has to be a grownup all the time. It must be awful."

"But I do break down."

"Not really. Not like I do. If you ever broke down like I do— You can't. Because then what would happen to me?"

It's dark; she can't see my tears. I feel good and sorry for myself. Poor Mummy. Poor old thing.

*   *   *

We secure our maps and, over lunch, plan two itineraries. If the heat continues, we'll head for the Tyrrhenian coast after Florence. If not, we'll stay in Tuscany and Umbria. Tomorrow, Venice or bust.

In the high old times, in order to enjoy trees, gardens, and open space, the Venetian aristocracy used to climb aboard special barges and retreat up the Brenta to the dozens of enormous villas that line this small river much the same way the imposing "cottages" of Newport line the oceanfront. Villas and cottages share also the same air of instant, rather than accreted, luxury. Each prodigality of stone, marble, statuary, and landscape is meant to outdo the rest, just as their Old and New World owners ruthlessly meant to outdo the rest in the sphere of commerce. Instant luxury, instantly available, and almost, as the longevities of great establishments are normally reckoned, also instantly abandoned due to changing times, left fallow or turned into tourist attractions.

Three years ago, the only spray-painted slogan I noticed in Italy was on the bulkhead of the Brenta where one of those enameled and cushioned barges used to tie up. *Nixon sei come Hitler*, it said, the X a swastika. Glad as I was they'd been on to the bastard, I worried about the spray paint, a medium too congruous with the splashy, affronting, anarchic side of the Italian character for the continued health of ancient monuments.

That worry is, here, all too realized. The long stretch of ornate wall surrounding Villa Nazionale, manifest champ of the extravagance competition and former playground of the powerful Pisani family, is covered with political slogans, mostly Communist.

Labeling the villa as a symbol of capitalist wrong seems redundant at this stage. On their own, the crumbling masonry, ruined gardens, algaed water basins, and vast, flaking gilt ball-rooms are sufficiently cautionary—demonstrating the evils not only of capitalism but also of vanity, envy, hubris, and the futility of laying up treasure on earth.

The abused river is foul with garbage; the rotting carcass of a large black dog moves sluggishly toward the sea where, tomorrow, we plan to swim. This river road was once the best route to Venice. Now the spending class of tourist takes the autostrada, so there's no money here for municipal grace. The natives are reduced to watching their unvisited attractions crumble, their garbage accumulate, and their neighbors rev varieties of engines. One neighbor, squatting bareass in a sparse, unprivate clump of trees, is masturbating. Ineffectively masturbating, without even the excuse of hard red emergency. How much more bored can a body be?

Grazie Madonna, the kid's laughing, only laughing, at him.

"*O! Tedesca!*" yell the sidewalk idlers. "*Fräulein!*"

"The next car that honks in my ear," she threatens, "is going to get a kick."

Redress for automotive assault comes definitively: we slip between the flanks of the cars and caravans that must wait for the next Lido ferry because there's room only for us. We roll aboard with seconds to spare, regally accepting the congratulations of the crew.

A hundred-mile day, often tedious because our new map has shown us routes that avoid not only *i brutti* but everything else, as well. True, when architecture resumed along the Brenta, so, too, did *i brutti*. But in the future we must strike a happier medium.

The best English-language descriptions of Venice are those of John Ruskin and Henry James, but be warned: once you've succumbed to their vision, your own is inevitably colored, secondhand.

Ruskin's kinetic paragraphs in *The Stones of Venice* struck Proust, for one, so forcibly that he was disappointed by the actual phenomenon of St. Mark's. It simply wasn't as pearled and jeweled and porphyried as the prose had led him to expect. The pen can also be mightier than the presence.

James sets you up for another kind of disappointment. A book like *The Aspern Papers* takes you so intimately behind those soft pink walls that when you turn from reader to tourist you're pestered by jealously. You *know* these palazzi—why does no one invite you in for tea?

It's best to visit first, read later.

Both Ruskin and James are elegiac. The former, indignantly: the Venetians had it all—a vital Christian faith and the good, beautiful things that organically flow from vitality rooted in strong faith—but they blew it, for nothing better than "the unscrupulous pursuit of pleasure." (The villas along the Brenta would abundantly qualify, for Ruskin, as unscrupulous.) James's elegiac tone works toward his thematic purposes, with city and fictional characters—to borrow Jamesian phrasing—vibrating to the same struck chords. Power in decline. Grace frayed by duress and privation. Noble beauty periled by expediency.

And should we be elegiac today? Opinion is divided. Certainly any existing sicknesses of society and the soul are unlikely to be redeemed in an environment so irretrievably linked to the demands and compromises of tourism. Put another way, people come to Venice only for beauty, which may not be reason enough for it to continue as a social entity. Added to these older problems are more recent dangers deriving from technology, progress. See Venice before it sinks, is the way that elegy gets written. Nearby industrial inferno Mestre drew so much artesian water from the soil that the wooden piles Venice was built on were exposed to the air and began to rot. (Wood will not rot if perpetually submerged.) Now that the artesian wells—some 16,000 of them—are off-limits to industry, the sinking should stop, assuming the sickness in the piles was arrested in time. But is this all? What of atmospheric corrosives drifting over from Mestre? And what of the worsening condition of the Adriatic?

Venice, as Ruskin explains, exists because of certain miraculous dispensations of nature. There is tide here, unlike other parts of the Mediterranean—just enough tide to rinse the city twice a day, but not so much that a delicate, open building style will require the ponderous interruptions of protective storm bulwarks or other battenings.

For over a thousand years, sea met city in perfect symbiosis. Now, with progress, the place is used harder every year. Whether the escalation starts with the wiles of the enticer or the appetites of the enticed is moot. What's certain is that progress allows no retreat and that the end of consumption is waste. How delightful will it be, in some grim future, to play among sewers rinsed only by a vaster sewer? (As it is, the inelastic wrinkle their noses and complain of the canal stink.)

Wandering down a quiet chiaroscuroed *calle*, these alarms recede. The city is too charming, too ostensibly intact, unspoiled. That rosy wall, those water-worn steps, will, forever, touch the same stretch of sunlit green water, timelessly giving observers this precise delight.

This false security holds because Venice, sinking, stinking, or not, is axiomatically and forever safe from the Visigothic invasions of the automobile. The minute we boarded the ferry, I felt the healing begin: *they can't get us here*. For a time, no insults to lungs, ears, nerves; any sexual confrontations will, without engines, be fair fights. Irrationally, since our *chevaux* must languish in the courtyard of our Lido pensione, we want the whole world to be like Venice. Whizzing around on small, open *vaporetti*—all other transport is clumsy and stupid by comparison.

*   *   *

Last night, and again this morning, I insist that my daughter keep her back turned on the city until we can enter St. Mark's Square at the Bocca di Piazza in its northwest corner. Because of the way boats run from the Lido, this involves nuisance and delay, but the reward is indisputable. We emerge from shadowy, hemmed-in, narrow obscurity to wide, dazzling space. All at once we possess the whole of the square, both its sublime vastness and the felicities of its composition. It is at this spot that the various elements of color, texture, verticals, and mass form their most magnificent unity.

We stand in a coma of admiration until sudden shrieks interrupt. A woman's shrieks, joyous, surprised—excited not, however, by this space or its monuments, but by the pigeons who have found her corn-laden hands. Pigeons whose acid droppings are inexorably, constantly dissolving the monuments, dimming their luster, pocking their smooth curves.

A friend of mine, a teacher of Italian who anxiously loves Venice, has sent generations of his students out into the world saying *topo piumato* (feathered rat) instead of *piccione* (pigeon). A scholar's ecotactic, worse than ineffectual because it displaces outrage with wit. And certainly here, this morning, there's no evidence of raised consciousness. The shrieking woman, her arms and shoulders so thick with beaks and wings and nervous red toes she resembles a particularly unfortunate intergalactic mutant, attracts a stampede of amateur photographers away from the far less fascinating opportunities of the monuments. We have to step lively or be knocked down.

When John was a little boy, his parents smuggled into Venice a suitcase full of horse manure. In the dead of night, they arranged it in naturalistic clumps just where the four bronze horses of

San Marco would have alighted had they magically become earth-bound and answered nature's call before cantering off on some occult errand. Days afterward the townspeople crossed themselves and wondered, was it a miracle? The papers were full of interviews, theories, signs and portents.

I relate this story to my daughter, who loves it—and instantly wish I'd kept quiet, for the telling makes me miss John in a new and sharply painful way. As we continue our sightseeing, I begin to hallucinate his long, elegant, loose-knit form wearing the evening clothes I've never yet seen him in, cutting like a slim, knowing blade through all this marzipan allurement—revealing the fine and true and delightful beneath these clustering and importuning surface blandishments.

But hold it. I'm the cicerone of this tour, not John. I can see and discriminate well enough on my own. What's up? Does the pastel, filigreed, water-lapped city, so richly feminine, make me pine for a man because I sense myself richly feminine? But why is he wearing evening clothes? And why are the kid and I peering wistfully into shop windows when we could be registering architectural details?

The shop windows here exceed even the usual high Italian standard of artful enticement. Mannequins are never used to display clothes—the shopper is tempted by pinned folds and unerring conjunctions of design and color. Tiny hole-in-the-wall refreshment stands lure us to spend with strategically placed dewy-cool goblets of fresh-cut fruit. Restaurant windows are heaped with poems of fish, pale clams, black mussels, tiny speckled squid, seaweed, fresh green leaves, and lemons. The vocabulary of Venice is not I see, I feel, but I want I want I want.

To be longing for a man is another way of saying I'm longing for that man's buying power. I *want*.

Before we parted, John told me his best Venice stories. He,

like Henry James, has been a guest at palazzi we can only gawk at. During their frequent visits, his parents always engaged their very own gondolier; one successfully taught John to scull with the long, fractious oar. While he ran through his stories we played lovers' games. What if he flew over to meet me at Harry's Bar? What if, next year, we slipped away, just the two of us, for a week? We'd stay at the Gritti—

To insert himself, he sent roses and filled my head with stories. He didn't, even to the point of ruthlessness, allow me my own Venice—one without him. So, docile as a lamb, I won't have it without him. It's no fun alone. Yes: ruthless. For him to mind less that I was without him in a favorite place of his, I had to be made miserable. His ghost here is far less tolerable than Adam's in the Touraine, for that was accidental, this deliberate. Around the thick icy sludge of this awareness licks hot anger— anger at the way love sets us up, at my docility, at the whole bloody situation. We'll never get away together, never. His wife, sandhill in the manger, will see to that. For the rest of our lives the most we'll have is the power to spoil each other's holidays.

The nice, clean pay beaches, in this sultry weather, are full. We resort to the public beach. The water is suspiciously warm, with soft brown globular seaweed bobbing nastily around. I wish it weren't soft and brown, that the water were colder. My daughter wishes the men's bikinis were ampler, their body hair sparser or at least less aggressively springy. And that their yelling, leaping, wrestling games were tempered by the tiniest demonstration of self-control. Down on men, I encourage her ridicule.

Something strikes her: "Why's the sidestroke the national stroke of Italy?"

"Tell me."

"Because the sidestroke lets them fumble. They never have

to wonder, underwater, if they're still all there. Pick an apple, fumble in the basket."

Fumble is her word for that characteristic brief caress Italian men bestow on their genitals every ten minutes or so. What's their real motive? Reassurance, as everyone mockingly theorizes? I've never gotten around to asking.

"Try it on your friend in Florence," she suggests.

"Assuming I see him." If I'm still this down on men, not a chance.

The public beach has three flagpoles. Today they fly the Italian flag, the dark red Venetian flag with St. Mark's golden lion in the center, and The Stars and Stripes. It looks so innocent and crisp up there that tears spring to my eyes. Tomorrow is the Fourth of July. I must rouse myself from my dependency funk to plan something to celebrate independence.

"Charming of them, isn't it? To fly our flag?"

"Like you say, when they're good, they're very very good."

No longer the angrily baffled ignoramus of our Early French period, the kid has laid down her preferences in artistic expression. Frescoes, provided she knows the Bible story; fortunately her school has daily compulsory chapel. Architecture she's gaining on. Sculpture is best of all, though she balks at art museums because she "hates" paintings. I have made this deal: if she will go receptively to the Uffizi and Vatican museums, she's exempt from the others, Venice's Tintorettos and Titians notwithstanding.

Other kinds of museums are fine with her. The Naval Museum, for instance, which celebrates the seafaring side of Venice that no longer exists. In this place we meet, on the Fourth of July, a quintessential American, a psychiatrist from Long Beach,

California. Like many people who listen for a living, he's talky off duty. In the course of his monologue, he invites us aboard the cruise ship *Golden Odyssey*, his home for twelve sun-filled days and moon-drenched nights. He's traveling alone, in more ways than one.

The *Golden Odyssey* is almost new, a pretty ship, in cruisebiz lingo, a mini-liner. Its purple, pink, and gold interiors are briskly air-conditioned. Around the kidney-shaped pool on the first-class deck other Californians lounge, reading Harold Robbins. They must be rich but don't look it; polyester is a great leveler.

Our guide whispers, "These people have had their money for a while, you know. I guess it shouldn't bother me—I'm a psychiatrist, I can afford to do whatever I want. But I still feel a little shut out, you know?"

We like him for this candor and pity him, too. How odd that he had the resourcefulness to seek out the Naval Museum—not one of your tourist biggies—but is blind to the message of polyester. Oh, California!

The printed plan of the day schedules "Anchors Aweigh" at one o'clock *sharp*. Boston Tea Party at four "in the Calypso Lounge." Dinner is formal, "the theme for tonight is, of course, RED, WHITE, AND BLUE!!!"

My daughter asks why no one is out exploring Venice, and is informed that many passengers will never leave the ship. "Or, if they do, they'll just talk about their shopping, what they bought. Last night I coaxed two couples into a gondola ride. They talked nonstop, never saw a thing."

I had hoped we'd run into an American on the Fourth, but not dreamed of such a lucky and corrective encounter. We've been taken to a high place and shown who lives there at $250 a day. Straightens me right out. I stop hallucinating John scattering lire to smooth our way. I stop thinking I want I want I want.

And—dare I say it?—my tooth has gone quiescent.

One final Venetian episode for the kid's education: we walk into the Church of the Frari where I anticipate a lingering session with the famous Titian *Assumption*. We've hardly blinked to adjust our eyes when out of the shadows shoots a woman, thick-set, powerful, dressed in widow's black, to strong-arm my daughter from her church. *No*, she repeats with each brusque shoving gesture, *no*—and nothing is more profoundly negative than that blunt Italian *no*.

Outside, my stunned daughter sags against the wall of the church as if facing a firing squad. It was her bare shoulders—she's wearing, this once, her sleeveless, high-necked sun dress without a shirt. She bursts into helpless tears.

Made the terrified object of random sexual whims, she has just been singled out by a representative of the church for cause and provocation. The door of the sanctuary has been slammed in her face. "You have to look at this," I insist. "If you don't understand why it was so upsetting, you'll be its victim forever."

"I don't want to understand. Why should I have to do anything? They do what they feel like to me—whatever they please. I'm through. I'm getting out of this perverted country. They can understand me for a change—or go to hell. I don't care. I'm getting out."

And when they're bad, they're horrid.

Chapter *Eleven*

Although it is time to leave Venice, we can't yet part from the sea and its promise of coolness, however illusory. We'll ride down the two long thin strips of littoral that enclose the lagoon and are connected only by ferry from the mainland, about thirteen miles in all.

Our plan is to eat a seafood lunch in the old-fashioned fishing village of Chioggia, but bad timing gives us, instead, a two-hour wait on the littoral of Pellestrina. A strange place, Pellestrina—sand-swept, desolate even in high summer, vaguely menacing. Locations for neorealist filming: life is hard and there are no simple solutions.

The villagers, like island people everywhere, maintain a distance from strangers. A noticeable number are lame. Others have a daft, half-witted look—inbreeding? We buy bruised and stunted peaches at a pushcart, cheese and bread in a dark, bare store. No hearty *mangia! mangia!* here. We feel as if we're disrupting a fine-tuned supply and demand system, robbing what is already allotted to others.

There are no trees, no real shade. We slump against the sea

wall with its rapidly shrinking shadow, too apathetic to climb up into the oppressive white heat and seek a swim. It is going to take everything we have to wait, to endure, with nothing to do and no one to talk to.

The kid yawns, stretches, abruptly goes rigid. "Oh shit—"

Two men on motorcycles.

They circle around, pull up, switch off their motors. In the silence, my daughter's stifled little whimper. For me, a disturbing flash: she's the one who's doing it—she's victim, flypaper, musk, *she's wrecking my fun.*

The voices of the young men reach me from a great distance. The soul of civility, they saw us on our bikes down by the ferry dock and wanted to meet us because of our *forza.*

We shake hands. Giovanni and Alberto. Blond Giovanni does the talking. He has the biggest bike, a Yamaha. Dark Alberto is decidedly the sidekick. Both are *vaporetti* operators in Venice.

They've known each other all their lives, having grown up right in Pellestrina, where they still live with their mamas and papas and sisters and brothers. Unmarried because not yet caught. "Us too," I play along.

Giovanni likes this. He's long pondered the differences between American and Italian women. An Italian woman thinks she must marry. American women understand freedom. "You and your sister are as free as men, and this is good."

These gross simplicities must stand. I don't have the language to shade them, to explain how some American women, yours truly, for example, do things in Italy they don't do at home.

Giovanni confesses to restlessness, discontent. Time for a change. Maybe leave Italy altogether. Go to America. His ironical laugh says, "like every other hungry Italian" and also gathers up the bleak American unemployment statistics we've already discussed, as well as the dearth of good bread, decent coffee, in the land of plenty.

By the time the ferry arrives, the kid's relaxed and playing too—pretending to be my sister and a college student. Before we leave, she has me ask why Italians like noisy motors. Giovanni answers with the same laugh that hedged the immigrant's hopeful dream of America. "The bigger the motor, the bigger the man."

The featureless Po Valley encourages reflection. How could the American flag over the Lido have looked merely innocent when I know my country is the *padrone* of the progress fever that might yet sink Venice? And how could my daughter have seemed guilty—whaddya expect honey, yer raskin furrit—in Pellestrina?

How can a liberal like me be vulnerable to the attitudes, no, the convictions, of the Amvets Lodge, the precinct house? My response to my daughter's terror at the sea wall seems infinitely more reprehensible than that of the Black Widow in the Church of the Frari. Travel broadens in curious and unexpected directions; life is hard and there are no simple solutions.

As a friend of mine once remarked, you don't have to be Jewish to love Ferrara—though De Sica is to Ferrara what Zeffirelli is to Verona, and the places made poignant by *The Garden of the Finzi-Continis* look mostly as you hope they will.

I love Ferrara because, after Venice, its serene, bricky buildings rest the eyes while its civilized manners rest the tourist-battered spirit. And because of Fabrizio's hostel.

Fabrizio, tiny and quick, with deep, expressive gray eyes, is famous among hosteling cognoscenti. Militantly anticlerical. Generous: if he has something you need, it's yours for the asking. (Asking is important. If you sneak even a dollop of oil from his hospitable larder, you'll get firmly and derisively put in your place.)

During the war he was imprisoned as an antifascist; his post-war period of socialist politics ended when he decided he could satisfy his idealism less abstractly as a hostel keeper. After twenty years of wiping international noses he remains unsentimentally persuaded of human decency—in the young.

"And what about the not-young?"

He shakes his head, smiles, gives me one of his long, fathom-less looks.

For supper, hostelers should go around the corner to the *pasta fresca* shop and buy some tortellini. Fabrizio will explain how to cook them *alla panna*, with lots of grated cheese. The pasta in this region is, most think, the best in Italy.

His friends in town are likely to drop in after supper. Everyone knows Fabrizio.

We have letters in Ferrara. Mine are from John, the most recent one mailed from D.C. Business has taken him out of town; obviously he wrote before he received my appalled early bulletins on Italy. This means no words of comfort or advice, and there's also scant correlation between his skeletal "more on this when I see you darling" style and my brocaded Venetian hallucinations.

This is too jarring and corrective to absorb entirely on my own, and I wait impatiently for the kid to finish with the thick heap of letters filling her lap. Her friends have come through royally, including Blair, twice.

His are on top, best saved for last and rereading, but she's staring thoughtfully into space instead of savoring them. Suddenly her hands shovel under the pile and up it flies, scribbled pages, envelopes, thin leaves of airmail blue. Next, tears. She's not the only one disappointed by her letters.

Do adolescents feel these letdowns more, or less, keenly than their middle-aged parents? Or is disillusion by definition adolescent and thus experienced uniformly from then on? I pull her to me and rock her, deciding not to say me too, me too—the last thing she needs at this point.

Apparently her friends are too "into themselves" for adequate response, whether to triumphs or disasters. Blair must have written immediately after hearing about the Maggiore grabber, but all he offered was this crass postscript: "Too bad you didn't have your hockey stick along!"

"It's worse coming from him. The others I understand. But Blair should be different."

"Of course."

"Really?"

"Sure. You give up more for a boyfriend than for other friends, so you expect more in return."

"And that's bad?"

"What do you think?" What do I? Bad to give up more? Yes, but giving can be sweet, very sweet. Bad to expect more? Yes. But bad to get more, no. Never.

She blows her nose, bends to collect the scattered letters. "I don't know about giving up anything. It's not like he owns me. Hardly."

This cool appraisal is so at variance with her customary dewy-eyed in-love submissiveness that I feel obliged to remind her she's renounced, for one thing, other boys.

"Yes, but that's not him. That's the school. If you dance twice in one night with the same boy, he's your boyfriend and the others stay away."

"My God. That stuff's still going on? Sounds like the fifties."

"Well, thing is, I have my little list."

She explains. All the girls at St. Paul's have their lists. Future options. Since you're allowed only one boyfriend at a time, you work through your options at a decorous pace. Breakups are emotionally draining, but, worse, if you're too greedy, move too fast, you'll be branded a slut. Even if each boyfriend in turn is offered, at most, a hand to hold and dry, closed lips to kiss, you'll be a slut. Fickleness is the determinant, not other behavior.

"What's the masculine form of slut?"

"I don't know. Party boy, I guess."

"Not so ugly a name, at any rate."

"Oh, the boys. They get away with murder."

"And if the girls copy them, they're sluts."

"Yeah."

"Does this have anything to do with the ratio? What is it—three to two? Okay, boys call girls ugly names to balance their disadvantage in the ratio. Artificially limits the girls' greater freedom to pick and choose."

She likes these ideas, likes them a lot. At St. Paul's, sandhill as any other boarding school, energy left over from academics and sports has been absorbed, during the years I'm familiar with, into the topic of Visitation. Under what conditions should boys and girls be allowed to visit in one another's rooms? Transcripts of earnest discussions on the question have been sent home to parents. A central and unspoken four-letter word drives the debate, but it isn't slut. Concepts surrounding slut, against such formidable competition, don't stand a chance of review.

Sudden, pelting rain, our only rain since the Jura. In our ponchos, dripping, we wait by the locked doors guarding the art treasures of Ferrara. Hard times have caused cutbacks in security staff and visitors must ring to enter each building.

The allegorical frescoes in the Palazzo Schifanoia cause me an attack of envy. All those fifteenth-century faces; such poised alertness to life's pleasant and multitudinous variety. Self-confident gentlemen in tights gracefully sit steeds dainty of hoof, ladies do needlework or gather in talkative groups. It is the dawn of reason, the dawn of infinite and delightful possibilities for the human race. No one is shown as isolated, moody, or neglected. Wit flows without the abrasive edge of malice.

How lovely to live in so affable an age. And how infallibly the mental habits of democracy appoint us courtiers instead of where logic would discover us, down in the mud with the fleas.

Leaping, as always, at any chance to honor a famous woman, I suggest a visit to Lucretia Borgia's tomb.

She used to be infamous, but the current line is that she was unjustly blamed for the murderous machinations of her power-crazed male relatives. Besides, the fancy footwork and vials of poison belonged to intrigue-ridden Rome, not to forthright Ferrara, where she finished the distance as an exemplary Estense wife.

Her tomb is guarded by a rigorously cloistered order of nuns. Unseen hands press buttons to release locked doors. A little wooden shutter flies abruptly open to deliver a description of the tomb in the language of our choice. As doors in progression click locked behind us, the kid's increasingly sure we'll never get out alive. This is even worse than Villa Santa Maria.

Fabrizio, that evening, thoroughly enjoys her round-eyed report. With high glee he informs us that the holy sisters are sprung from the cloister every election day. "To scale down the Communist margin. Too big a Communist victory is embarrassing for the Pope."

Fearful of the Apennines on my first bike trip, I clung to the Adriatic coast as long as possible, which means I've experienced Rimini, a resort that makes Miami Beach look muted, low-key, undiscovered. (The seashore of Fellini's boyhood, Rimini, where earthy Saraghina dances for the boy Guido in *8½*, resembles Pellestrina.)

This time, veterans of the Alps, we will confidently barrel down the spine of the lesser range, skirting Bologna. Not only is this straight line the shortest distance between Ferrara and Florence, it includes one of the most beautiful passes in Italy, della Raticosa.

My previous route, which I recommend except for Rimini, was an homage to Piero della Francesca. First Urbino, the concisely steep city of Federigo da Monfeltro, that consummate Renaissance man who early recognized Piero's genius and sat for several of his notable canvases. Next Sansepolcro, the painter's birthplace, a golden, green-shuttered town tucked against the Alpe della Luna and the home of his sublime *Resurrection*. Finally Arezzo and the glowing frescoes in the Church of San Francisco, where earthly and divine elements are held, celebrated, in perfect balance. With Piero you are not left, as in Vézelay, confused about the management of your flesh. God is good and so are his gifts, including the gift of sensation.

We will follow the vigorous Idice up to its source near the pass. (Italian is precise in such matters: the Idice is not a river but a *torrente*. The Po is a river.) Our route begins auspiciously with a *castello*, a toyshop one with a square, crenelated tower, establishing a motif of enchantment that seemingly will hold right to the gates of Florence.

The beauty of these mountains is more gentle than majestic; all level land is cultivated, mown green alternating with the dark gold of ripe wheat. As we climb under the bright afternoon sky, a ground haze ethereally surrounds and makes footless the salients below. Against just such landscapes, fourteenth-century painters placed actors in Biblical dramas. I can easily visualize Mary and Joseph and the Babe fleeing into this utterly Tuscan Egypt. (As a literal-minded child up on her Near East geography and plant life, I found these transpositions disturbing. Someone was playing a trick, taking me for a fool.)

We are joined by a cycling club from Bologna astride splendid silvery bikes. The men slow their racing pace to our laden one. Giorgio becomes my partner. My daughter and Franco are out of sight ahead. Franco, Giorgio assures me, is a *bravo ragazzo*, a good guy she's perfectly safe with.

The club rides here four afternoons a week, quitting where the downgrades cease and the uninterrupted ascent to the pass begins. Giorgio tells me this in a mixture of French and Italian very easy to understand. He is in the business of selling camping equipment. Though the French market is nearly saturated, Italians are just getting into the swing of outdoor life. His store supplies everything: "Stoves, tents, fishing gear—"

"Pedalboats?"

"Yes, certainly, many small boats, sleeping bags, clothing— excuse me, your clothing is not right. You should wear these pants. No underpants. Underpants are bad." (He wears, like every European I've ever seen on a ten-speed, regulation cycling shorts, stretchy black knit, with a chamois crotch.)

"But already they laugh at us for riding men's bicycles," I protest. "If we wore men's pants—"

He brushes this away. "They laugh because they are stupid. Italian men are stupid."

Riding like this is, as Giorgio points out, companionable. We pay no attention to cars, unless their excessive honking inspires counteroffensive repartee. When Giorgio discovers I'm the mother, he switches from signorina to madame. He applauds our Simplon feat in French and Italian, but something worries him. "Excuse me, but you do not ride correctly. You should never use the large front sprocket uphill, never. This knots up the thigh muscles and makes them tired."

I ride as I do for psychological reasons. Instead of using all ten choices in mountains, I ride as if I had five and an ace in the hole, a second wind to summon at will. Who knows how steep this baby is? And for how long? With no reserve, I'm beaten before I dare investigate. I can't manage to explain, and Giorgio natters insistently on about it, so I give in, do as he says, gearing up on the rear sprocket to compensate.

He is right, of course. Male, he understands and exploits the machine's full capabilities. Female, I've struck a bargain, made a deal, psyched out the situation and fit machine and self into its imperfectly presumed givens.

That his approach, this time, is correct makes a good argument against the sexual separatism some women promote and more men, especially in councils and boardrooms, practice. Not all machines are as benign as bicycles, though, and other times my approach will be right. Making two good arguments against separatism, as well as two good arguments against the wholesale capitulation of women toward that boardroom world of male thinking. The differences between the sexes are too potentially helpful to be blurred; androgyny is a fake salvation and a boring one. If Piero della Francesca could hold earthly and divine in balance, we ought to be able to balance male and female.

When our friends turn back to Bologna we feel lost. Before long, with continued, and steeper, climbing, this translates into fierce hunger. Frassineta, the only village in miles, is too tiny for a grocery. We venture into a trattoria—one spacious, unadorned room with high rafters, worn wooden floors, and a half dozen tables, most still covered with forests of empties not yet cleared from long ago lunch. Some lunchers haven't been cleared yet either. The place is the local hangout, and in this season the crops can grow unwatched.

When I describe our predicament to the signora in charge, she offers us spaghetti, salad, and bread. And impressive kindness, this. Flexible to the point of sloppiness in other matters, Italians are adamant observers of mealtime rituals and five o'clock is definitely not a proper hour for supper.

One of the good old boys at the table near the door has overheard our story. While we wait to be served, he tells it to whoever drops in. Each time he starts out the same way: "They are not Germans but Americans."

Despite this interest in us, we're thoroughly eclipsed by the signora's granddaughter, about a year and a half old, just awake from her nap. All gather closely around to squeeze chubby arms and legs, to yell, inches from her baby ears, full-throated endearments and cries of admiration.

My daughter, always grouchy and tender after sleep, is shocked. The poor baby! Then she has an insight: noise is love. Italians are conditioned from birth to be noise addicts—which is why they keep upping the dose.

The spaghetti is good, the salad, *rugola* from the signora's garden, is sopping with dark, rich olive oil. We recklessly order a second liter of mineral water, currently our favorite thirst quencher. *Frizzante, fresca*, hang the cost, signora.

She asks if we've had enough to eat, and although we could easily handle seconds, I'm reluctant to put her to any more trouble. Since I'd noticed, earlier, a box of handsome peaches in the kitchen hallway, I order two. This causes mild consternation. She sits down with us and thinks hard. "Do you want a big peach, like this" (her hands a foot apart) "or little peaches" (chopping motions) "fried?"

Bewilderment, until I realize I've asked for *pesce*, fish, not peaches. Significantly, though, she hung right in with us. Kept from her granddaughter and her *riposo*, still she hung in. I fully believe she'd have whistled up a village boy and sent him over to the Idice to hook us a trout, if fish was what we had in mind.

Once, in the hilly campagna above Florence, my friend the bicycle champion caught, with his hands, a little gray trout. He cleaned it, built an economical fire, and cooked it between two forked pieces of wetted greenwood, held chopstick style. Two delicious mouthfuls each. Recalling this, I decide. I will look him up. Of course I will. A man who can catch a fish with his bare hands—

Our bill is well under four dollars.

The Passo della Raticosa, 968 meters, lies luminously apricot in the late, slanting sun. Cars pass rarely; the wide, peaceful loveliness is untouched by development of any kind. For some time we've been scouting for water, intending to sleep where we find it, but drought has left the spillways parched and full of rough weeds.

After the pass, we shift into automatic pilot for the downgrade, listening intently for water—and here it is, icy and clean, tree-lined for privacy, with a hayfield, the innerspring mattress of sleeping out, adjacent. We strip and bathe in the leaf-broken light of a fat, bright moon. The best day of our whole trip— sportive terrain, unsurpassed beauty, good people, free bed and bath.

I intend to establish this firmly. "Best considering it's wretched and despised Italy?"

"No. Best period. You love to make me admit things, don't you?"

Yes.

Chapter Twelve

In terms of our own cycling effort, the major difference between Alps and Apennines is that the latter's grades, though steep, are shorter in duration, less arduous for us than the Jura were, though improved conditioning may be a factor in that comparison.

After the Passo della Futa, our enchanted route's second pass, it's mostly downgrade. A swing around a tight bend reveals beloved and familiar Florence spread out far below, Brunelleschi's dome massively, excitingly dominant. A stupendous feat, they say, of structural engineering, but for me the true audacity of the dome has always been its skin of tile the color of an unripe persimmon, sharply scored by ribs of white marble. The effect is fresh, witty, and right—*giusto*—which are also the qualities of Florence. I can't wait.

The folks at the Pensione Cristallo are a chilly lot, but the signor does remember me and produces for us a bed and a place to stash *le bici*. His wife and her mother, as before vigorously protest allowing *le bici* in the house. *Non è giusto*. We are outlandish and crude to expect such a thing. What next? As before, the women are overruled by the signor and left, by him and by us, to mutter among themselves. I'm home in my favorite city; their dark looks are nothing to me.

After lunch, showers, and short naps, we go to blow our minds with the Palazzo Vecchio, splendiferous demonstration of Medici brains, taste, and energy. What a family—art, science, botany, geography, politics, music, and the money from fiendishly adroit banking to indulge these enthusiasms as succeeding generations took them up. In Florence, to describe the Medici, you thumbnail a meaningful line alongside your nose: damn smart cookies. Their portraits show a tendency toward mouths expectant and receptive, but ironical at the corners. Always a promising combination.

In the Palazzo Vecchio's richly ornamented apartments, Catherine de Medici's sadsack-to-vindictive career as the Queen of France seems freshly incomprehensible. How could the daughter of Lorenzo il Magnifico be a chronic also-ran? And why were her sons such losers? One of history's odd puzzles.

Part of the palazzo is Florence's city hall, the entrance guarded by a matched set of cutiepie *vigili urbani*—here, as in every Italian city that attracts tourists, the city cops are selected and costumed to be part of the aesthetic whole. I ask one of them how to look up my friend's phone number. Before I can stop him, he's touched his helmet and dashed off to find the man. To find him! All I'm prepared for is a phone conversation. And here he comes, Etruscan as ever, smoking a Marlboro in a great display of cool and naturalness. We shake hands.

I introduce my daughter who was clearly expecting someone more dazzling, a man more on the lines of the *vigili urbani*, the kind of Italian a mother could be expected to lose her head over.

He invites us both for dinner that evening. I accept for myself only, perfectly all right with everyone. Though the kid'll have to spend our first evening apart locked in her room with a picnic—for even in the City of Flowers, *brutti* lurk—this is decidedly the lesser of two evils. *Il campione*, she knows at a glance, is one of my experiments.

We dine up in the hills, at the same rural trattoria where we wept farewells three years ago. Prompted, he admits I startled him by turning up so unexpectedly. When, years ago, he received my letter about Adam, he forced himself to understand he'd never see me again, but perhaps, since I am now traveling without him— He falters, but gets it out: are we still together, Adam and I?

Some instinct limits me to yes, certainly. "And you? Have you found other Americans?"

Meant jokingly, this produces a glum response. He has no one, no one at all. He has "white nights," is, these days, far from happy. A promotion has brought increased responsibilities, not much more money. The work is often dull. He's sick of Florence, fed up with the superficialities of city life, city people. His wife, I will remember, is a city woman. No, nothing new there, no change for good or bad. The children are well. He'd like to take them and move to the deep country, where his mother lives. Where the old ways still prevail.

My daughter's parting shot was, don't forget to ask him why they fumble, but I can't possibly. We are on terms too formal. I do mention, without specifics, our bad experiences on the road. Not surprised in the least, he cuts me short with a weary sigh. "Lucky you're not rich or they'd kidnap you, cut off your ear. Italy is changed."

"What about this new president?" (After much parliamentary stalling, yesterday they elected a Socialist who was a resistance hero during the war.)

"*Brava Italia*. The man is eighty-one years old."

"But the Communists approve of him?"

He smiles. "I remember. You love the Communists."

"The hostel keeper in Ferrara told me they were the hope of Italy."

A cynical laugh. "A Communist is fundamentally someone who believes in divorce and abortion. Or more money for less work."

He launches into a long, sour, self-justifying complaint of municipal malfeasance involving opportunistic gaming by so-called Communists. I lose the thread among the idioms and must fake sympathetic indignation. "*Non è giusto,* absolutely."

His sourness distracts and worries me, but I hesitate to point out, you, too, old friend, have changed in three years. I suppose I'm afraid he'll lay it at my door. He's already made me guiltily uncomfortable by showing me all my letters—my short, feeble, illiterate letters—in the special gold and red embroidered silk case he bought for them, to carry them, not next to his heart, but close: in the glove compartment of his car.

Besides sour, he's fussy. He picks at his food and informs the politely concerned waiter what he can and cannot digest in hot weather. His features, as he elaborates these details, soften and relax. Ah, I think, a happy subject. I talk about the *pasta fresca* in Ferrara, the mistake with the peaches and fish (which doesn't amuse him enough to suit me), and describe our fortunate discovery of *acqua minerale frizzante*. He shakes his head at my credibility. "Most of it is fake. They add carbonation at the bottling plant."

"I don't care, it works. Let's go, okay? I'm pretty sleepy."

Aware that tomorrow is our last day here, he invites us to visit Fiesole with him, morning, afternoon, whatever we like. Cowardly, I stall. I'll call him tomorrow, after checking with my daughter. "She wants to see the medieval football—is it possible?"

"Tomorrow night is the final match. It will be sold out, of course—but I can get tickets through my connections."

My bad conscience transforms this generosity into a bribe, which I quickly rationalize: if I'm going to spend time with him tomorrow, might as well make it easy on myself so it's easy on him. I then suggest we skip Fiesole and meet instead for an evening picnic before the football.

"It's fun, no? The football?"

"Fun for the tourists."

Sour bastard, I irritably think, and am still thinking when he pulls over, switches off the engine, and takes me in his arms.

An astonishing experience, to be touched by a man after weeks of nunnish, arduous, preoccupied insularity. Immensely without warning, a wild clamor obliterates *i brutti*, fatigue, motherly niggles—and, strangest, my dismayed dislike of this man whose hand is thrillingly on my breast. Sex, for me, begins always in the head, but live and learn. The clamor must be served. The sly treachery of the flesh. And its glory.

My daughter and I have had a wonderful day, skimming the sightseer cream at breakneck speed, a pace that suits her and for once doesn't frustrate me since I've already lingered and ruminated in Florence. Big hits: the Botticellis in the Uffizi, the Boboli Garden, Vivoli ice cream, and David. David literally opens her eyes, all previous nudes having been studied through the scrim of her demurely dropped lashes.

At the Uffizi, in front of an unknown master's *Visitation*, she stopped cold; it's a word she had believed limited to the school context. When I explain that Mary is visiting John the Baptist's mother, both women pregnant by divine intervention, she loves it and begins to construct an intricate, naughty link: alibis for virgins. The joke is finished off by Tintoretto's *Leda and the*

Swan. "The holy ghost is a bird, right?" "Well, shown as. A dove, usually." "Okay, between doves and swans, which alibi do you like best?" Best I like you, I say obviously, though not aloud, because you're learning to make jokes, learning not to be afraid of links.

Now, bone weary, we prop ourselves against the balustrade of the Piazzale Michelangelo to wait for *il campione.* I've assembled the picnic; he, presumably, will arrive with the football tickets. He's late, which is not at all his style. My daughter is growing peevish, anticipating a dull evening of being left out of the conversation.

"I said I'll translate."

"Sure you will. The way you always do."

Her peevishness irks me less than my acceptance of *il campione's* bribe. I wouldn't mind calling everything off, going to bed early. Below us lies the panorama of Florence and its surrounding green hills, the view that Isabel Archer, still a free woman with wind in her sails, saw from the terrace of her future husband's home. "Look at the light on those river houses," I coax.

She won't. Tired of looking. "How long do we wait for this guy? I'm starving."

We nibble at the picnic. After ten minutes, we stop nibbling and tuck in. When he's forty-five minutes late, we devour his share. Somewhere in there we confess out loud that we both hope he isn't coming, screw the football.

The instant the food is gone, we exchange quick, complicit grins and bolt for freedom. Giggling hysterically, we fly down the steep, shrubbed path. Is the coast clear? We slither around a corner, duck into a doorway. Our eyes are peeled. They'll never take us alive.

Outside the football arena that has been set up in the Piazza della Signoria, we are caught up in the mob, finding ourselves in a pocket of attractive American kids. My daughter discreetly cruises them, marking out the preppies. No one my age in sight; people my age have reserved seats. At a signal, apparently, we'll be free to shove our way in without tickets, to stake out standing room wherever possible.

Magically, someone shouts my daughter's name. A schoolmate, with two other young men, also schoolmates. All three older, more sophisticated than she, their trip a graduation present. Hugs and screams. As she comprehends that here, at sorely tried long last, are real people, people she can actually *talk* to, her face turns a rich, humid pink. Her eyes shine violently blue and wide. She may levitate.

They've opened the gates. We burst into the arena.

Up on the scaffolding, our perches are tenuous and uncomfortable, but the view is unobstructed. Torches flame dramatically on the parapets of the Palazzo Vecchio. My daughter's face flames under the sheltering arms of her friends-who-are-boys— and not vanilla, I note. She looks about five years old. We've missed the parade of horses and banners, but are just in time for the entrance of the teams.

The game is a free-for-all kind of soccer. Tackling, eye-gouging, slugging, kicking, kneeing, and biting are allowed and cheered. When a fight breaks out, members of both teams pile on until no further movement is possible. A bell rings. The players who can still stand regroup and the ball goes back into play. No one wears padding. Concussions and broken bones are ordinary.

Pretty soon I've had enough. I leave the kid to her friends. It is pure bliss saying, in effect, I leave you to your bliss. Luckily the boys, too, depart Florence tomorrow in the graduation present car, and luckily they're heading north. Otherwise I think she'd be tempted to cheat, to hitch a ride for just a little more talk in her own language.

At the pensione, no message for me from *il campione*. In a few days I will write to him, presenting our side of the story and adding that I hope he wasn't held up by some misfortune. He will never answer this letter, I predict. The mystery will never be solved. Maybe he couldn't secure the tickets after all and was shamed after his bragging talk of connections. Maybe, in the morning light, his importunate flesh mortified him: he has that finicky streak. I'll never know, but the mystery will keep his memory green forever. Did he intend this?—to lodge, like a thorn, in my memory? Perhaps. So I'd think twice before carelessly popping in on a man who'd saved all my letters in a gold and red embroidered silk case.

If a helicopter set you down, blindfolded, ears plugged against dialect clues, you could still tell where you were in Italy by other distinct regional differences. The shape and texture of the bread, for example. We've eaten through the Frenchy crusts of the lakes to the twined biscuity "couples" of Ferrara to the dense, moist graininess of the robust Tuscan loaf.

I've begun to wonder if sexual acting out is also regionally determined. The motorcycles of the north have been superseded by trucks and truck drivers. First, contact and flanking. Invitations, comments, blasts on the horn mark this phase, along with raunchy sibilances from the airbrakes. Then we're left behind. When we've heaved our sighs of relief we find, over a rise or around a bend, the truck, parked half on the road, half on the shoulder. At the tailgate stands the driver, alone or with his co-worker. Cocks are out, erect, aimed. As we pass there's laughter and shouting and slow, raking pivots of the weaponry.

What's it mean when a man so savagely mocks the part of his

body made for pride and delight and generation—the future, that is, of his line and his people? Of all the disturbing things we've witnessed in Italy, this, to me, signifies real trouble. These men are, literally, degenerate—away from generation—for clearly they intend to mock and abuse their own hopes and traditions as well as to shock and scare us. Am I overreading? I don't think so. There's nothing playful or flirtatious or enticing about their maneuvers. Rather, they seem desperate defenders of the last ditch, so frightened themselves that I am afraid to appear other than what they bargain for. I am afraid to laugh at them, funny as they seem the third, fourth time.

Alberto Moravia has said that the greatest possible human suffering comes when we feel the cultural foundations we count on inexorably giving way beneath our feet. *I brutti*, this suggests, are suffering, are acting out against pain and confusion, and it's not hard to guess that one thing giving way is the dependable, comfortingly frozen position of Italian women. Women are not behaving. The church, formerly their chief ally, the definer and defender of those fixed womanly virtues, can't make them behave. Is not allowed to try, for these new women dare to ignore the Vatican and, instead, march on the Quirinal, demanding divorce, demanding abortion, demanding equal treatment with men. By riding around like this, we salt the wound, demonstrate the reality of womanly freedom. To make it worse, we have come to enjoy the *relics* of masculine vigor, power, and genius; like everyone else, we're aware that Italy is, today, bankrupt, in disgrace, gelded. The realms of action and conviction seemingly have been appropriated by terrorists and kidnappers.

Recently I met a woman who teaches at the University of Rome, an American married to an Italian economist she met square-dancing when they were both students at M.I.T. She too believes Italian men are feeling seriously menaced by changes in their women. Her own example of retaliative degeneracy was the way her increasingly conspicuous pregnancy caused an escalation of harassment. This in the country where the Madonna and all babies are—were—esteemed to the point of idolatry.

And the effect of so much exposed cock on my timorous daughter? Curiously good. An approximation of what I hoped Italy would do for her. She yells fluently back—not at the truck drivers, because I've warned her they're a special case—but other roadside idlers get as good as they give. Flip and brassy, she shouts insults, and then, out of range, laughs wickedly. "Did you see their faces? I really zapped them." She especially likes a fatty: "*O! Pancia! Bómbola!* How's the wife and kids?"

She orders food and drink with new authority. She saunters around bearing no resemblance to the hunched, quavering victim of the lakes region. Partly it's the result of unburdening herself to her friends in Florence and having them take care of her, protect her, remind her of all those charming and normal patterns between women and men. (Yes, of course we can protect ourselves, enroll in karate classes. But I suspect we will always seek and be comforted by emblems of male protection, as long as we expect to bear children. Dress rehearsals for the big event—the months or weeks or, if we're tough, hours that some man will be needed for protection since we're too occupied with vital business to protect ourselves.)

But the main reason for her change is, as she put it, "These guys are such total assholes, even the dumbest thing I could ever do looks good by comparison." Unruly Italy has taught her what I attempted to in faraway France, that she'll never see any of these people again and it's a golden opportunity to try new moves, risk mistakes and clumsiness, open up. Going back to Switzerland, which at one point seemed the only solution to *i brutti*, would never have done the trick. Switzerland would only have provided more practice in the sandhill gentilities she already has by heart.

Her new ease extends to me. My own moves and risked mistakes no longer fill her with scorn or doomed embarrassment. Instead, this kind of pure music: "You really know how to handle yourself. No one messes with my mummy."

"Must be my arrogant carriage."

"What?"

"Adam. He thinks I have arrogant carriage."

"I like Adam."

"So do I."

"What's going to happen when we get back?"

"Depends whether he's let mealybugs get at my grape ivy."

"No, really. What're you going to do with these two guys?"

"Have to wait and see."

"Will you tell me?"

"Sure."

She considers. "Not arrogant. Chic. That's what's amazing—you can still look chic in that same old skirt and top."

"Thank you. You look chic too, in that same old dress."

"I do?"

"Uh huh."

Too pleased, she sprints ahead. She's so laid back she can almost bear to believe my compliments. We've come a long way. Shaping up for a happy ending.

I catch up. "Listen, I have to tell you something. John is married."

She's shocked. She doesn't get it. "Don't you feel like an absolute shit?"

"I don't like it, if that's what you mean. If you mean, do I feel like a thief, no, I don't. It's not much of a marriage."

"Why doesn't he get divorced then?"

Because men like John don't divorce without a woman to go to and who knows if I'm a woman to go to yet, certainly not me. "He's got kids."

"So what?"

"You know. Hanging in for the sake of the children."

This sandhillism is the dumbest thing she's ever heard. "No one ever hung in for my sake."

"That's true."

"I mean, if my father left me their father can leave them. Can't he? Doesn't it make you mad? It makes me furious."

Ah, but furious at what? This fresh evidence that marriage, the end of the movie, her own chosen destiny, is difficult to impossible? Or furious that she must be forever the child of a broken home—a fate these others, John's kids, unfairly will escape? Broken home: I hope the concept confuses her. I hope she's too straightforward to deny that, the split accomplished, each parent's home appeared intact in ways the original uneasy emulsion (through which her father and I listlessly dog-paddled) did not.

Assuredly, much broken-home trauma is activated and sustained by social forces which have vested interests. In the past, absorbed by unwieldy doubts and passions, willfully determined that the children's lives run smoothly, I had dismissed the bad effects of such pressures as I dismissed the source of them: benighted sandhills of the worst, most repressed type, grinding their species' axes at our expense; fuckum. A survival point of view, but one I forgot to re-examine. It's now obsolete. More confident of my own direction, I can afford to pay some attention to the hurts my daughter apparently feels, regardless of source. I have, I realize, evaded this issue. But no more, or she's likely to remain stuck, on the edge, like a "liberated woman" who cannot cease cherishing and savoring past injuries where identity, or at least a significant share, is rooted.

"You ought to have your head examined. First you complain Adam isn't committed, and then you take up with a married man."

"Yeah. Chronic access problems. I said, I don't like it. I like to be proud of the things I do, and I'm not proud of this one." Not in the abstract. In the particular, another story. "The way I read it, I'm not taking anything away from his wife that she wants." Her ocean view, her BMW. "I'm sort of helping her out, even—she's not too big on sex."

"She isn't? Really?"

She's incredulous, frankly incredulous. A good sign. Interesting presage. If not conclusively a happy ending—must do something about that taste for vanilla—unquestionably a happy beginning.

Chapter Thirteen

The unrelenting heat dictates the design of our last days. We're passing up Siena, Assisi, Perugia, quitting to hit the beaches. I've heard good things about the Tyrrhenian seacoast, and if we don't like it, the mountains just inland reassuringly crawl with routes colored scenic on the map.

Between Florence and the coast is a diversity of terrain remarkable even for Italy. First a steep climb with views of olive groves and Flights into Egypt, then on to Tuscan hill country—romantically perched castles surrounded by Chianti vineyards—and then, suddenly, widely, Kansas. Wrinkled up into hills to fit, but Kansas nonetheless, nothing but ripe golden wheat for miles until we see, high against the sky, the long massively fortified profile of the Etruscan city, Volterra.

This open, hot, windy region ends at the Cecina River. We follow its green shade to the sea. Five distinct regions in one day, in only eighty miles.

Eighty miles in killing heat. As much as the topographical variety helped, the real prod to continue was the promise of long, cool, saltwater soaks. I have decided that saline flushes will heal my poor fork—somewhat illogical, this, because the salt of my sweat excruciates. The villain is the padded vinyl saddle my bike came with. I should have replaced it.

The subject of bike saddles concisely illustrates what goes wrong when the sexes don't communicate. From the beginnings of cycling, the best saddles have been narrow and made of hard leather, the idea being that the force of your pedaling isn't diluted by any springy bouncing up and down. These physics are reinforced, of course, by machismo—"only sissies want soft seats." Women who complained were dismissed as whiners, allowing themselves to be so dismissed.

During the cycling boom of the early seventies, as more and more women bought men's ten-speeds, the industry "solved" their complaints by introducing the padded vinyl saddle. Only recently, as if by accident, did someone discover that a woman's pelvic bones are spaced differently from a man's so that, just where the traditional leather saddle curves upwards, a woman's bones require something flat. Simple as that. There is a new leather saddle that supposedly accommodates this anatomical difference—but even a traditional one is better than this vinyl stupidity, bone distress being far less demoralizing, less of a piece with the whole dismal sociology of female troubles, than tissue distress.

At the coast, where no museums or cathedrals make demands on our consciences, we finally go lax, go on vacation. We're also sure we can't possibly need all our money, and begin to spend more freely in restaurants. At one vine-shaded *cucina casalinga* garden we order ravioli and are served a slick eggy pasta crimped around a delicately seasoned ricotta and spinach mixture. These little turnovers, in shape exact replicas of *chiao-tze*—Peking ravioli—remind us that before Marco Polo came back from

China, Italy had no pasta. At a waterfront restaurant linguistic imprecisions bring my daughter an enormous filigreed mound of tiny deep-fried squid. Her new adventurousness permits one crunchy taste, which sells her. She eats enthusiastically until the edge is off her appetite and previously held squiddy concepts— slimy, suction cups, sci-fi killer monster—take over. She falters and drops her fork. I spear a few. She tries again. It's a fight to the finish, stop-and-go ambivalence right to the final pale pink tentacle, but that she tried the first bite, given the narrow band of her food preferences, is a major breakthrough.

"I'm remembering the year you ate vegetables," I say. On her fifth birthday, that divinely malleable year of childhood, I made her a deal. She would eat the vegetables served her for a full year. Afterward, to eat them or not was her choice; I'd never bug her again. The first few months she gagged theatrically, rolled her eyes, clutched at her windpipe. Then she settled down. At supper the night before she turned six, she cleaned up all her peas, an event by then commonplace.

"Then what?" (This is the part she loves.)

"Have you eaten a pea since? A single pea?"

"Nope."

"Have I bugged you?"

"No."

"Two women of conviction and honor."

"Why did you make me eat them?"

"The rest of us lived on vegetables. It was a drag cooking special meals for you. And a drag defending those special meals to my mother. I thought that after a year you'd like everything and my mother would stop casting freighted looks around."

"Oh, your mother— Your mother was weird. Tell me about your glasses again."

"I couldn't see the blackboard and the school nurse sent a

note home that I needed glasses. 'I know those nurses,' my mother said, 'always so alarmist.' I begged and pestered until she let me go to the eye doctor. When he agreed I definitely needed glasses, she said, 'Well, if you get them, mark my words, you're going to wear them.'"

"And you've never taken them off since."

"And I've never taken them off since. Seeing is nice."

"Why was she like that?"

"She didn't believe in doctors. Unless you were bleeding buckets and making a mess on the floor, you should let nature take its course. Only spineless weaklings and alarmists go running to the doctor with every little twinge."

"Which is how I almost died."

"Which is how you almost died." She was just under two, with a bad cold. That morning I had given her orange juice and an aspirin as I had for the preceding five days or so. A friend dropped in for coffee.

"That baby's very sick," she said.

"Just a cold," my mother's child serenely replied.

"Has she seen the doctor?"

"No, of course not. It's just a cold."

"But look at her eyes. They're so strange."

Alarmist, I thought, but looked—to see my daughter vomit. A great rush of rusty fluid.

"I'm starting my car. You call the doctor and have him meet us at the hospital."

I obeyed, although even at this point I felt hesitant. So much drama. Wouldn't regular office hours do?

After a wait of an hour and a half, the doctor reappeared. "We think she's going to make it." They'd pumped her stomach. She must have eaten, on her own, a half bottle of aspirin—the adult kind. She had pneumonia. Was in an oxygen tent.

"By make it, do you mean live?"

That's what he meant. "You got her here just in time."

"What's wrong?" my daughter, alarmed, asks.

"Nothing. I was remembering. It was a narrow escape."

I'm not prepared to tell her that I have just understood, for the first time, that while she didn't die of my mother's unwisdom, my mother herself did. My mother died of not going to the doctor until it was much too late and she was far too weak for the interventions of medicine and surgery that would have saved her. I've "worked through" the sorrows and rages of both illnesses. I've recalled again and again the sight of my baby tied hand and foot inside her oxygen tent, tubes taped to her arms, to her nose. Felt again and again the impotence of watching her cry and not being able to go to her. Doctor's orders: "If she sees you it'll upset her more—she'll want to get out." And again and again I've relived that stiff suspenseful moment when I sat by my mother's hospital bed staring at her thin, waxy hand, wanting to clasp it in my own but restrained by the rules that had rigidly governed all the years of our separate lives. We do not touch. It's a rule. More, I'd been boycotting her for several years, and this made us horribly shy with each other. *Take it*, I ordered myself, and when I saw her hand yellow and slight in my strong sunburned one, I dared expose my tears.

She, too, was in tears. We do not touch, and we do not cry, but I saw her cry; for once I saw her plain. She was, after all, flesh and blood, not the uncanny eminence of my imagination. A flesh and blood woman, no longer young, dangerously ill, who hoped she would recover and live.

The clarity lasted only a naked, breathless second, but when it was over and formality had resumed, I had forgiven her for never letting on how she felt about me. How she felt about me, against the release of that forgiveness, that blissful release of ancient resentments and baffled rages, was simply not important. Later we could get around to me; we had time for that and a host of other questions later.

I never saw her alive again. And never until now have I linked her death with my daughter's narrow escape. The collision of these two events stuns me. Fast on its heels, fresh and hard, is the knowledge that my mother really is dead and gone and nothing can ever be done about it or those unasked questions.

So when my daughter, alarmed, asks what's wrong, I've had to say "nothing"; I can't trust myself with more. When I'm able to discuss this experience with her, I'll remind her that one problem with human procedure is the way we wake up in the morning to find ourselves mothers or fathers before we've recovered from being docile daughters or sons, obedient to the errors and traps of the past.

As soon as I can trust myself, I'll begin. Not waiting too long, because who knows how much time there is?

The sea is transparently clean, with just that edge of chill required to seem healthy and sportive. Between the sea and the road are long stretches of well-kept public land, shaded dramatically by umbrella pine. Sixty or seventy feet tall, these trees are attractively, oddly, sculptural, especially when a big yellow moon rises to silhouette them against the night sky. Frequently we pass people crouched beneath the pines, sifting through their fallen needles with delicate care. They're searching for *pignoli*, pine nuts, we learn, and we're given a recipe. Grind up a good handful and cook lightly in olive oil with garlic and chopped fresh parsley and basil. Serve this *pesto* on linguine with grated cheese.

We stay at several campgrounds on the shore. One is uncharacteristically expensive, which means we can observe a classier assortment of vacationers than usual. Almost everyone here is Italian. Campsites are well-equipped, causing me to remember Giorgio from Bologna and my daughter to remark, as we shake corn flakes into our ricotta containers, "At least they 'match.'" (Before this trip, I never heard her put quotation marks around anything.)

Real books are being read, instead of *fumetti*, the photocomics favored elsewhere. There is a remarkable absence of recreational yelling. But the major difference between this campground and others where we've stayed is the American facilities. Unlimited free hot showers, a by-product of the solar desalinization process that supplies all but the drinking water. A coin-operated washer-dryer, unprecedented in the campgrounds, towns, and cities of three countries. Bowing to tradition, the management has also installed sinks for hand-scrubbing, but how can a woman lose herself in the suds with that infinitely more efficient, not to say chic, cyclops staring her down?

Most ominously, this campground subverts the customary and merry generational mix: you can get rid of your kids by farming them out to Baby Camping. Baby Campers have their own sleeping pavilion and counselors who arrange games, activities, and swimming sessions. Kids and keepers alike wear navy sweatsuits lettered "Baby Camping" in white. Their American prototypes are so familiar to us that it is some time before we realize this lettering is not in Italian but English.

Italian families, voluntarily segregating themselves on so flimsy and arbitrary a basis as age? The tireless, cheerfully drudging *nonna* disenfranchised by washing machines and pert hired keepers in navy blue? What next? We needn't wait long for the knell of doom. In the well-stocked store—the whole place is as conveniently arranged and spanking clean as any American could desire—the bread, soggy of crust, comes wrapped in plastic.

The name of this campground is Parc Albatros. There seems to be, this season, no escape from bird analogies. In Coleridge's poem, which, like millions of other pre-TV schoolchildren, I once memorized, a Mariner, sailing mid-ocean, slays an Albatross, pretty much for the hell of it. Strange and terrible punishments follow, and after his fearsome ordeal, the Mariner must wander ceaselessly, stopping "one of three" to tell his tale and its lesson: nature is good and should be revered; affronts will bring nightmares of retaliation from which there is no escape.

Near Civitavecchia, where leftists, antifascists, and Jews were imprisoned during the war, the sea begins to stink. It is low tide, and children pick their way across algae-covered rocks to play in the unpleasant water. Up on the cliffs above the highway— we're forced to use the highway, this stretch—new houses are in various stages of completion, promising intensified assault on a shore already gasping for mercy. The children, oblivious, squeal and splash. My daughter imitates the ceaselessly warning and scolding mothers: "Stefano! Francesca!" She thinks it's nice that people have time for long names, "even for kids."

We ride through the resort town of San Marinella—palms, pink and white oleanders, and an architecture that campily combines the worst of the Art Stucco twenties with deliciously vulgar contemporary medium-rise. Via Aurelia, so nobly named, is going to provide us a flat and ignoble entrance into Rome. We abandon it and head for the inland heights.

Ten minutes later we are in rugged country—high, rough pinnacles, mountains stretching into the endless distance, game preserves with, unfortunately, locked gates, and, far below, the sea glittering silver. The road is too steep for us, even at this stage of our conditioning. We've already pedaled sixty miles and we're hungry. But it is exhilarating, after the flats, to be up where we can see something, and we decide to press on to the campground at Lago di Bracciano, fifteen miles away.

This round, mountain-nestled lake, about six miles in diameter, is a scant twenty miles from Rome. I expect the worst— Maggiore, only more so—worries confirmed by the town of Bracciano, whose main street, cobbles steeply tumbling down to the lake and its massive, cliff-hanging, guardian *castello*, is a river of strolling and bored soldiers from the nearby army post. There are thousands of them, some gap-toothed and stunted, some tall and wonderful. We are too great a novelty to pass without uproarious notice—extravagant pantomimes of longing and desire, shouted invitations and questions. We haven't the strength for them and flee, bouncing along the cobbles, forgetting to notice the castle, forgetting we planned to eat supper here.

Once out of the town, the lake is so tranquil and unspoiled a traveler could starve. I say we ought to go back, but my daughter, of the breathing leather saddle, won't hear of it. The soldiers. The upgrade. Either alone, argument enough.

We stop to take our bearings. It is dusk, and the castle bulks commandingly against a glowing rosy sky. Lights shine below along the shore. The campground?

A uniformed man parks his car and approaches us. He is very correct, very handsome. Proud of his English, which he delivers in a half-shout. "That is not *campeggio*. That is installation of the Italian Air Force. I am major in Italian Air Force. You are German? American? Impossible. Why do you go with bicycle?"

"Why not?"

"You must go with car to see Italy. Bicycle is old-fashioned."

"We are old-fashioned people. Over two hundred years old."

He can't be kidded. Sticks to his point: we should go with car.

"Please, Major, where is *campeggio?*"

"*Sempre diritto.*"

Just as I suspected, he hasn't the foggiest. In the past two days, we've been stopped three times by *carabinieri.* Now the major. Clearly, this region's roadside sex takes the form of official questioning. We're near Rome. Seat of the church, of government; once the power center of the entire civilized world. You bet. Therefore, the sex is highly, appropriately, sublimated and ritualized. Instigators wear uniforms, get off on papers, interrogation.

Found, the campground is well worth the search—a small, clean gem tended by a man about my age. He's too gentle and sweet to be as burdened as he seems by long-standing sorrow, but then, who said this is a just world? Later, in the tiny waterside trattoria, eating the plates of indifferent spaghetti and excellent salad he's served us, we chat with him and catch inklings.

"Your *campeggio* is the best of our whole long trip."

"*Grazie.*" A smile of heartbreaking sadness. "But the *campeggio* is not mine. I am only the manager. Everything here belongs to my father, everything. The trattoria too. Your salad comes from my father's garden. He is seventy-five. I am forty-five. His only child. I work for him."

"You are a very good son."

At this evidence that we have understood, he beams. He then adds that he is a bachelor and his mother died a few years ago. It's just the two of them and their endless game of seeking and withholding. I feel a certain rapport with him as I would with any superannuated child still waiting for Them to approve. Though my wait never made me gentle and sweet.

His name is Emilio. When his young friend Luca appears, we're introduced. Luca, improbably vanilla, is exactly my daughter's height and age. She's instantly smitten, thrown into disarray. Shyly, in English, Luca answers my questions. He's a Roman. Stays up here in his own tent while his parents are in the city. They come up on weekends and live in their caravan.

He's responding to my questions only, my daughter being closely occupied with using the tines of her fork to measure the checks in the red and white tablecloth. How am I going to bring the two *ingenuosi* together? I've scored, manner of speaking, on this trip; it's her turn.

A half dozen noisy little kids charge in, demanding ice cream. Luca waits on them, Emilio busy in the kitchen. Suppose I initiate a flirtation with Emilio—but no, I go too far. Some *ingenuosi*, like holy hermits, should be left alone. But: "Let's stay a few days, okay? Get to know the place a little? Talk to Luca about Rome? He can really help us. It's such a huge city, and I don't remember it at all, really—"

"Would you please cut that out?"

"Come on. He speaks English. He's preppy. What more can you ask for?"

No more. It's already too much. They are so ideally suited that they have to separate at once, scuttle away from each other in paroxysms of adolescence. Further intervention on my part will only embarrass and enrage her, and we're out of practice for a fight.

Wherever Luca pitches his solitary tent, it's not near us. Our neighbors are pleasant middle-aged Dutch and German couples, all insisting we're fools to pull up stakes so soon. To be, after a single night, two girls getting on their bicycles and riding to Rome, Italy.

"Rome is stifling."

"Terribly expensive."

"Noisy and rude. You better stay with us."

"You should leave your tent here and take the bus down for

the day. You'll be glad enough to come back."

We wake, for us, late. Even so, no one is stirring but Papa, the old crab, picking and eating figs. The campground is part orchard. Next to our tent, undetected in last night's dark, stands another fig tree, heavily fruited. Greed prompts me to ask him if we may have two. He gives me a hard look before assenting. Scrooge.

There is nothing like a ripe fig right off the tree—thin-skinned, sweet, crunchy-juicy within. (The crunchiness changes, after picking, to mush—figs, in their way, are as fragile as sweet corn. Both should be eaten before they catch on to the fact that they've been severed from their source.) "Let's stay another day," I beg the kid, "if only for the figs."

But we can't. As we check out, Luca watches from a distance. I should have been more forceful. Or wily.

Papa is watching too. I thank him for the delicious figs. "Take more. Fill your pockets," he surprisingly says. But we can't do this either. I feel like Masaccio's wailing, expelled Eve in the Florentine church of Santa Maria del Carmine. We must leave Eden empty-handed. *È giusto.*

I ask my daughter if she remembers the fresco. She does. Feels that way too.

"Okay, we're going back."

"No!"

It's Luca. She likes him too much. Won't be able to stand leaving him. "We'll never get to Rome at all if we go back now. Don't you remember the cuties in Dijon? Every time I think about them I still feel like crying."

"But Luca *lives* in Rome, Furley. He can come with us, show us around. We'll take the bus together, the three of us."

No. Never. It's too dangerous. Too close to every romantic

fantasy. By the time this is sorted out, our Rubicon is behind us, and we're near the gates of Rome.

She crosses the city line first, flinging her arms high overhead in the victory gesture of bicycle champions the world over.

Chapter Fourteen

"I can't get over the size of the cars."

"I can't get over the filth. Much worse than Italy."

Home less than an hour, we're walking along Cambridge Street, doing re-entry errands. Cambridge Street is a kind of sump for the hospital and government complexes it connects. Here gather weirdos, drifters, wheeler-dealers, pols, and patronage beneficiaries. It's a hot afternoon and people are wearing as little as possible, us too.

My daughter grabs my arm. "I just realized something. We're in shorts and halters—and I'm not scared. It just hit me. We're surrounded by men, and no one's going to do anything to us."

Took the words right out of my mouth.

People ask, "How was your trip? A success?"

"Fantastic," I say.

That's usually enough. Everyone's happy with a happy ending. Some want hard data. How far in all? (1800 miles.) How far per day? (60 miles, average.) Cost per day? (Close to ten dollars each. Yeah, I know, but food is outrageous.) Lose weight? (Some.

Less than the kid.) Flat tires? (One. There's no broken glass in the roads, even in Italy, insouciant Italy. Deposits on all bottles, so they never formed the habit of recreational smashing. And another thing. We could leave our bikes on the street anywhere, locked only to each other with a light cable lock. No one would steal them or strip them or rummage through our panniers. Nope, not even in Italy.)

"How did it go? A success?"

Everyone loves a happy ending.

The Victor Emmanuel happy ending is a present for Adam because he believes in art-as-alembic.

This story begins ten years ago with my first Roman visit. I set out one morning to find Michelangelo's Campidoglio, which a Rome-loving friend had assured me was one of the most beautiful piazzas in the city. Partly because of having no sense of direction, but mostly due to my unformed sensibilities, I ended up instead at the nearby Victor Emmanuel monument. Sore-thumb conspicuous, a wedding cake in the shape of an old office Underwood, you can't miss it.

I reverentially climbed its chalky neoclassical steps (my friend had mentioned steps) and lengthily studied the equestrian statue of the king who—it seemed incredible since even the clothes are wrong—I assumed to be Marcus Aurelius. And I selected two of the knottily muscled nineteenth-century extrusions on the steps to be the ancient Dioscuri, Castor and Pollux of (my friend said to notice) the wondrously star-struck gaze.

Several years passed before I discovered my mistake; it still embarrasses and warns me.

This trip, as my daughter and I were studying Trajan's Column, the monument Ultra Britely hulked in the middle distance. Very casually I asked her what she thought of it. She instantly declared it awful, "gross" in both the teenage and standard senses.

"Not only that," I conclude pridefully to Adam, "she produced definitive reasons why. Quite articulate about scale and tone."

"Is the grossness of the Victor Emmanuel monument so subtle?"

He's laughing at me. He toured Italy once and found the country entirely resistible. "It's more surprising that you made the mistake than she got it straight. How could you?"

"How can anyone do anything? How could you let mealy-bugs murder my grape ivy?"

"Fantastic."

"It was her first trip, right? Is she going to be a traveler like her mother?"

Or anything like her mother?

Well, yes and no. In Florence, in the Medici Tombs, is Michelangelo's *Dawn*. Massive thighs; weary, anguished face. This woman has gazed deep into the eye of the beast and is not entirely sure she's survived the encounter. However, her great physical strength—she could handle the Simplon easily—suggests she has a fighting chance. Also, it is dawn. The night is past.

This is the kind of happy ending, I tell John, that I can have confidence in. Sandhills achieve happy endings by denying the beast, or by imagining they've caged it—but the only way to cage it is to cage yourself and pretend you've done the other.

As a result of our trip, my daughter has begun to recognize the negative consequences of caging herself. She's learning to tolerate ambiguities, to stand, sometimes, on sawdust, to accept the fact that the beast is at large and will always be at large. She may even have fearful intimations that sometimes, after a night of meeting its uncaged eye, she'll be left, like Dawn, unsure whether or not she has survived the encounter.

She was always too intelligent for the simple and narrow view. Now she's too experienced as well. You can't, as they say, tell kids anything, but you can show them plenty. She's been shown. The splinters of multitudes of pesky and ambiguous truths are festering; the long, slow process of understanding without lies, labels, and delusions has begun. Corrupt, she has a chance of survival. My job, as I see it, is to continue to remind her that although festering truths hurt they sometimes create antibodies that heal. And also, not incidentally, she has, like Dawn, physical strength, which is bound to increase her odds.

I discuss these ideas with John because if we begin to love each other seriously we will also have to summon the strength and courage to love ambiguity. Not only because he's married; that's almost the least of it. Suppose he weren't married—the destination, the Rome, that shapes our love would still be ambiguous and unconventional, since that's all I trust in the way of happy endings.

One of the smarmiest ideas of the late sixties was that the young can teach us so much, if we'll only let them. A corollary piece of smarminess is that our children should be our friends.

In Ferrara, during and especially relaxed moment, I carelessly remarked to my daughter that it was interesting how well we got on together, considering we weren't really friends.

"Not friends? What do you mean, not friends?" She was upset and angry, unwilling to hear my backing-and-filling explanation—that a friend is a peer who can reliably do for you what you reliably do for him or her. Calmer, she accepted this: we each have friends in number, but I have one daughter, she one mother, so let's concentrate on discovering what that means to us.

For starters, we decided a mother should ideally be a hidey-hole, a fixed star, someone a kid can count on for love, acceptance, practical advice, hot meals, warm beds, especially when the others, the friends, fail. A support system that draws no taxes from the kid. (That I slide past "acceptance" so easily shows I am persuaded that my custody fight against the sandhills is ebbing, that I don't envision having hypocritically to applaud alien values forever.) Then, still ideally, when the mother requires the support system, usually because she's old and frail, the kid, still without tax revenue, does her bit. In the middle time, we have to figure out how to keep this ideal free from its most common perversion—we don't want to be stuck with each other only when no one else will have us, when we're at our lowest and worst.

Our Ferrara conversation aside, my daughter has, in unsmarmy truth, acted as a friend and even as a teacher to me. I intended to redeem my failings as a parent. What unexpectedly happened was that my daughter untangled me from my own mothering. Being with her this summer put new wind in my own sails so that I'm running free in latitudes where I once banged futilely about in irons.

One Roman morning, half-awake, I played with imagining her father's multiple reactions to this bald, unexplained announcement: the trip worked, she's corrupted. Sitcom kept dissolving into dream and daydream. Somewhere among the sequences it occurred to me that my mother, young, unwary, totally unprepared, was confronted by the beast—all at once, in its fullest, most appalling measure. The first lucid moment that followed, she swore her children must never guess a force so primordially dark existed. The deadening, limiting concealment began, with demonstrations of affection and love immediate casualties. Love lulls, softens; it could not be risked, though of course she acted from love. It was to maintain this constant, unblinking vigilance that she began to keep herself and her feelings secret.

No. Nice and tidy, but no. My mother had her problems, I have mine. It is sad that we suffered our bouts with the beast separately when we might have huddled shivering together. Leave the rest. Stop knotting threads. To explain all is not to forgive all. The moment in the hospital by her bedside stands. The rest is trivial, born of bandit cravings for happy endings.

My daughter and I are at Cape Cod, on her day off. She is again baby-sitting for her sandhill family—to wind up the summer, to compensate for the parched days when she couldn't swim, and, probably, to make up for the beast.

Not every subject is freely permitted, but more than enough are, including marriage. Why, she's asked, since I'm so "militant," did I ever marry in the first place?

I laugh. "People did, then. We asked, why marry this man or that one, but not why marry at all. Different now."

So, why did I? In such reckless haste? Not, as her employers have confided to her they did, to investigate the human heart in close, secure quarters. In fact, for opposite reasons. I overvalued, and at the same time greatly mistrusted, love. Rather than be tormented and torn in two, I married to dispense with the subject altogether. Did I love? Was I loved? Absurd questions: I'm married, doesn't that settle it? Let's move to matters less loaded. Let's build a house. Dig a garden. Have a dinner party. Join a country club.

Loving is being there. Marriage—the framework of marriage—is getting there. In those days I hadn't the courage for bicycle trips or other slow, arduous explorations that give practice in being there.

"...and they say both partners have to work hard—together—to structure a life both can believe in."

Her employers. I take grudging issue with the self-help manual language but nothing else. They seem, her family, to be pulling it off. And the children, with their sweet, open friendliness in and out of the family circle—"If you judge a tree by its fruit, those kids certainly prove someone's doing something right."

"Well see? So don't laugh at me when I say it's what I want. It's the best life I can think of."

Don't laugh, and don't cry, either. "One love, forever and ever. I wish you well. I'm skeptical, but I wish you well."

"Maybe it won't work out. But don't forget, I've got time going for me. I can try stuff. I'm not in any hurry."

After word

It's been over twenty years since my daughter and I took the trip that became the armature for *Happy Endings*. Both of us live in altered circumstances, as people used to say in quainter times. And of course cycle touring has changed, too.

Before Telling All, I must take something back. Wearing a helmet in no way signals to cars and trucks that they possess superior rights to the roadway. No right-thinking cyclist has ever picked me up on this point, which is a bit surprising.

My moment of conversion came when a friend called from the hospital. Like me, he'd thought helmets were for people who checked under their beds before risking sleep. Now he was under observation because he couldn't remember how he came to be lying on the road next to his bike, which had been totaled.

I bought my first helmet and started working on everyone else. My daughter balked more than her brother. Hot, she complained. Itchy. Plus, they smoosh your hair.

So does a cranial cast, I riposted. "And if either of you kids turn yourselves into broccoli by riding bareheaded, don't expect me to come visiting. Except maybe once, to yank your plugs."

Crazy-parent extravagance, when used sparingly, tends to convince. Eventually my son found his own rationale, nothing crazy about it. Between orthodontia and his Ph.D., he figures he's spent more money on his head than any other part of his body. His conclusion: "Gotta protect my investment."

Long-distance cycle trips, in the seventies, were unusual enough for me to imagine I could sell a book about one. The agent at Curtis Brown who'd had no luck placing my first book, a novel, thought my name too obscure to try for an advance contract. Seeing my disappointment, he reminded me that we weren't taking the trip just so I could write about it. If the book didn't pan out, we'd still have our memories.

Yeah, sure, I muttered. Once I was well into the writing, however, I could see that he'd offered more than a palliative, that my comparison of being there (the bike experience) with getting there (the experience of the car) extended to the book biz. Writing is being there, publication getting there. Lacking a contract, I felt free to tell the story exactly as I pleased, no inhibiting influence seeping in from the publishing side. Many writers I've known refuse to "work on spec," as they dismissively put it. But having tasted these astringent freedoms first time out, spec still seems to me a good way to go.

The first editor offered the manuscript rejected it. "The author's parenting methods are too unorthodox to attract readers in quantity," her letter explained. Chilling, but within weeks, Houghton Mifflin had said yes.

I didn't use my daughter's name on purpose. We had different last names; she could stay under cover if she wanted. Answering mail from readers curious about her reaction to her portrait, I'd quote her own summary: "I get trashed for being a brat, which I was, a lot of the time. I come through in the end, so it's fine. Anyway, no one knows it's me except my friends and people who, you know, *know*."

Especially for a first-time author, the book was a critical and financial success. No end of admiring reviews came in from all over the country. Anatole Broyard, a man whose thinking had been important to me since college, wrote that it "ought to become a Bible for modern mothers and daughters." There was a good paperback sale, and a German translation earned such nice royalties I began to have complicated feelings for sassing the Fatherland in print.

Three different movie options followed. Though none reached filming stage, the casting offered its own interest. For *moi*, sequentially, Joanne Woodward, Linda Lavin, Dyan Cannon. This last choice brought me to a stunning realization: beneath my mild-mannered exterior an intelligent blond bombshell yearns to be born. Kristy McNichol, a name in those days, was cast as the daughter with Linda Lavin. Otherwise this role was to have been taken by Joanne Woodward's real-life daughter, then Dyan Cannon's, which is also to say the daughters of Paul Newman and Cary Grant. Heady stuff! The kid loved every minute.

Fast forward to the early eighties. My daughter has graduated with a B.A. in American Studies and the Nellie P. Elliot award for "one of the finest athletes ever to attend Yale." She doesn't look like me, except around the eyes when we're grinning. More precisely, she's a knockout.

But where should she begin living real life? She's tired of Boston. New York's bloodsucker rents promise tight, shared quarters and other grim tradeoffs. Some of her friends have ventured into the Sunbelt, with particularly good reports coming from Dallas. When an international bank with headquarters there offers her a job, she takes it.

Soon after she's settled in, the Dallas Yale Club hosts a party for The Game. On the big-screen TV, Harvard's ahead. The invitations said to wear school colors, so the kid, like several others, has shown up in her letter sweater.

A tall, beefy Texan, late fifties, hoists himself into her personal space. "Hey, little lady," he says by way of greeting. "That sweater belong to your daddy? Or your boyfriend."

"Neither," says the kid. "It's mine."

Sly twinkle. "Whajja get the *letter* for? *Mud* wrestlin'?"

Her laugh, she'll swear to me later, has no edge. The moment strikes her as weird but primarily comic.

Tex demanding an answer, she plays it straight. "Actually, it's three letters. Field hockey, squash, and lacrosse."

His reaction is lost in an outbreak of cheering. Yale has intercepted, made 15 yards on the play. As the offense runs onto the field, Tex says, "Nice to know you" and moves on to work the rest of the room.

Early Monday, her boss tells her he's just hung up from talking with Tex, who'd called to sing the kid's praises. "Which is how I found out," she subsequently tells me, "that he's on the bank's Board of Directors."

"My God," I say. "What luck."

"Luck?"

"You didn't punch him one for insulting you. I would've. Verbally, anyway."

"But Mom. He was right out of central casting. You don't take guys like that seriously."

I love this story. Whenever it crosses my mind, I laugh aloud, feel like a good mother. And, for all my aversion to labels, like an effective feminist.

My daughter has reached the age I was when we took our trip. Apart from the chronological coincidence, are there any similarities between her fortieth year and my own?

Certainly there's not much that's immediately obvious. Because she didn't rush pellmell into marriage and babies, her children, a girl ten and a boy six, are too young for alpine crossings. She's raising them not alone but with their attentive father, the husband she likes and loves. Me too. He's not remotely vanilla, and happily ever after wouldn't surprise me a bit.

While my various employments were, and continue to be, provisional, my daughter has a career. She left the bank after three years to become a developer of large projects: a new Sunbelt courthouse; a mixed-income apartment building in Manhattan; adaptive re-use for a proud but defunct nineteenth-century brewery.

She's not only good at this work, her energy—athletes *do* have energy—is prodigious. When her husband decided he wanted to go to medical school instead of continuing on as a reporter for the *New York Times*, she was able to shoulder most of the financial burden along with making Halloween costumes and gingerbread houses.

Her aspirations for ocean frontage are unrealized and, she says, unmourned. Tabled, I'd put it: this is America. For now, it's an expanded farmhouse in a town that hopes suburbia won't smother every last rural remnant. There's no BMW in the garage, and no SUV, but let's leave it at that. Brand preferences, among buyers who are grown up, don't reveal character.

Her values, her concerns, are close to the ones that preoccupied me at the time of our trip. My granddaughter shines on the soccer field, dazzles on ice skates. The most popular girl in her class is a mall rat, a clotheshorse who utterly scorns everything athletic. So *boring*, she'll groan, getting no argument from her courtiers, including my granddaughter.

Materialism, in short, has reared its predictable and herd-forming head. My daughter and some of the other class mothers worry about the destructive "messages" communicated by the pint-sized cliquemeister. Shopping isn't the main thing, it's the only thing. Cool rules. A cutting putdown will trump any form of kindness. And never forget: whenever I want, I can decide I don't like you, and the minute I do, no one else will like you either.

We've all *been* here, the mothers wail, why can't we *stop* this stuff?

Since I've been there too, in my own girlhood, and so have most of my female friends and relations, I wonder if our DNA makes inevitable this kind of thralldom. I'm not worried, though. My granddaughter can't wait to be old enough to cycle from Paris to Rome with me and, probably, her mother. What worked before will work again.

Besides, the base looks solid: This is a household that's trying to keep life's getting and spending aspects in proportion. "We live in a privileged world," my daughter observed in a recent e-mail. "I'm constantly compelled to remind the kids that most people don't have what they do. There's a soup kitchen they work in through their school's community-service program. This helps them understand, but a few hours a month isn't enough to make the necessary impact. We have to figure out ways to get them involved with the gritty locales beyond our tidy community."

I live in a tidy community myself, these days. It is a considerable distance, in several ways, from the Beacon Hill attic where my teenaged kids and I, with mixed success, managed our enforced intimacy.

Several years after he surprised me with those roses, John, whose real name is Charlie, accepted the realities of his marriage and moved, alone, into an apartment a few doors away from me.

This change made both of us much happier, which is not to say we took it at all lightly. We did what most people do—tried our best to minimize the bad aspects and keep faith with the good. Charlie's children, parents themselves now, show abundant signs of having forgiven us for the turmoil the divorce obliged them to endure.

Forgive and forget, the saying goes, as if they were equivalent. Forgiving is active, difficult, and worth every struggle because its outcomes are so fundamentally desirable. Forgetting takes us unawares, sometimes to our loss. Since each of us gets only one history, why not cherish every chapter? Because the memories are so painful? I think the name for that strategy is repression. Forgive and forget might be a condensation. It might have been forgive so you *can* forget, unshackled by toxic residues like self-justification, bitterness, and resentment.

Speaking of toxicity, our determination to stay clear of marriage was an important compatibility. It helped that no one worth bothering about (except my poor father) took phrases like "living in sin" to heart. Even so, once I'd moved out of my apartment into Charlie's, I ran into the perdurable and sexist assumption that we weren't married because I "couldn't get him to commit." He came up with an adorably gallant stake to drive through this one's heart: "I keep asking her," he'd say with a sad shake of his head, "but she won't have me."

After a decade of this we did get married. In secret and primarily to circumvent the Commonwealth's confiscatory estate taxes. Two years later, when we were sure marriage hadn't changed us, we went public with the non-event. Some of our friends made amazing fusses. Our kids seemed pleased. My father relaxed.

*   *   *

An early order of business was to go bike shopping. Though Charlie hadn't cycled since school days, he took to it right away.

Boston is a good cycling city, once you surmount its lunatic driving style. (The stop sign is merely suggestive.) Looping the Charles River is a gloriously scenic bikeway that brims with human interest. Another bikeway extends from Back Bay station to the Arnold Arboretum, which, in every season and weather, remains my favorite place in the entire city.

Over time, we covered most of the good cycling routes in Massachusetts, Vermont, and Connecticut. One adjustment for me: Charlie won't camp out: "Had enough of that in the Army." I, of course, insisted he give it a try. Once was enough; couples must pick their conflicts with care.

In 1980, we cycled abroad together for the first time. Charlie's company had offered him the splendid gift of a three-month sabbatical; we spent most of it in Eastern Europe, which was new to both of us. No one in the world, at that time, had any inkling that the Iron Curtain might be other than eternal. We ran into food shortages—in the harvest season!—and had difficulties finding lodging, but a heavier burden came from traveling among people forced to live without hope, their legacy from the mistakes of Yalta.

After that experiment, we stuck with the easy West: three tours in Italy, two in France, one in Spain, one in Portugal, and one that combined Holland and Belgium.

Except for Portugal, these trips were do-it-yourselfers; for temperamental reasons, we resist the pros and their increasingly glossy brochures. The promise of these outfits to do everything for you tends to undermine the best aspects of cycle touring, not least its egalitarian cheapness and easy contact with local people. In Eastern Europe we learned to use our bikes to penetrate state-sponsored xenophobia and the most opaque language barriers. Portugal showed us how readily this ice-breaking capability gets lost when cyclists show up in a group.

What about the mechanical support offered by the pros? And their "expertly researched" route maps? As anyone who has made a self-guided trip—or, for that matter, enjoyed *Happy Endings*—knows, these props are hardly crucial. Depending on them instead of taking a few risks and improvising solutions of your own makes it harder to come home with new or refreshed self-confidence. That said, a case can be made for letting someone else provide the bike you'll ride. For sheer, inert clumsiness, nothing beats a bike packed to meet airline rules, and every metamorphosis of vehicle into baggage and out again can be counted upon to test the do-it-yourselfer's nerves.

In between our travels, we worked pretty hard. Charlie's venture capital firm specialized in small, start-up companies, and their growing pains filled his days with unpredictability. I taught, first at Boston University, then at the Harvard Extension School, and started writing mystery novels.

Charlie was, and is, an ideal first reader. I hand him finished writing with complete trust. If he doesn't get something, it isn't there, on the page, to get. He is generous with appreciation and an inspired accomplice during the writing process. *Deathampton Summer*, my first mystery, drew on bedrock sensibilities: Charlie's family had been summering in Southampton, out on the East End of Long Island, New York, since the 1870s. And when I was drafting *A Killing in Venture Capital*, he never complained about the way our dinner conversations kept being hijacked by my demands for technical detail.

Sunny Jim, his mother would call him at especially fond moments. She died much too soon. That she liked me and took obvious pleasure in my company did wonders for this monadnock's daughter.

*　　*　　*

I was finishing my fourth mystery when a good friend asked Charlie, then past sixty-five, when he was going to retire. "No idea," he said. She pressed on: "How many men lie on their deathbeds wishing they'd spent more time at the office?" Kingdoms rose and fell while Charlie considered. "Good point," he finally said.

Beacon Hill was an ideal location for a breadwinner determined to walk to work. Once retirement made this key consideration irrelevant, our tolerance for city noise and bad air weakened fast.

We had a ready alternative, because Charlie had inherited his mother's house, a fifties ranch near the center of Southampton Village. Though the yard was small, there was room for a garden.

We could grow our own food. For me, this would be a realization of a long-deferred dream that irresistibly combined practicality, self-reliance, and romance.

Ironically, in light of my daughter's youthful aspirations, an equally important draw was the ocean, five minutes by bike. Nothing I know, not even an afternoon in one of Boston's admirable libraries, is as reliably restorative as surf swimming. If the sea happens to be too rough, a pleasant half-hour ride delivers Peconic Bay, calmer and warmer. My ritual is immersion before Memorial Day, no quitting until Halloween.

The tidy communities of the East End are incessantly battered by the environmental pressures that come with popularity. Fighting back, trying to preserve what remains of our rural distinction from Sprawlsville, U.S.A., seems more urgent to me than writing mystery novels. I managed to complete my fifth a few years after we moved; its successor, after two drafts, still lacks legs. Call it tabled. (It's America here, too.)

I still write, but not fiction. My op-ed column, Local Slant, runs every other week in the *Southampton Press*. I like this work a lot. Whenever readers want to discuss a column with me, I like that too.

Subjects for the column rise out of the same bafflements and enthusiasms I used to sneak into my mysteries—questions about the human condition, the choices we consciously make, and the many so-called choices that get shoved down our throats, largely by advertising, largely so that others can profit from our susceptibility. Each of my mysteries has a character, for instance, often a main character, who cycles as a matter of course. Just as with kids, you can't tell readers anything, but you can show them plenty. I tried to show that cycling was an efficient means of transportation and fun besides. When I use my column to promote bikes, or to raise questions about habits and behaviors that are destructive to the environment, I don't have to sneak. I can be as direct as I was able to be, it has just struck me, in *Happy Endings*.

However altered my circumstances, then, I seem to have come full circle with writing—to have regained amateur status, in the original sense of that phrase, with all the satisfactions felt when starting out twenty years earlier. This is a fine place for a writer to find herself in.

So much for work. About life's other great need, love, I am much less cagey than I used to be. This is Charlie's doing.

Kinship ties are scarcely mentioned in *Happy Endings*. Now I have friends throughout Charlie's large extended family, and I've grown positively tribal in my reliance on my own two brothers and their wives, my sister and her husband, and the niece/nephew generation. We laugh, sing (fifties pop, bel canto, Cole Porter), draw comfort from each other's company and the peculiarities of our common history.

My gifted, brave-hearted son, a chemist who deserves his own book, recently did our italophilic family the great favor of falling in love with a woman of Italian descent. She's a biologist. For months she'd come home from the lab and sit down to her sewing machine. When she finished her wedding dress, she started making her attendants' dresses.

Love, then, is abounding. I love having a garden. There is no downside to having a superabundance of asparagus and raspberries. Nor is there any downside to having grandchildren. Yes, it means you're getting older, but unless you were dead, you'd be getting older anyway.

Add rafts of dear and funny friends, a son-in-law who can hold the tenor line in family quartets, and a daughter who says she wants, with her own children, as good a relationship as she enjoys with me, and I sometimes have to pinch myself.

Best not call it a happy ending; I'd hate for anything to end. "I've got time going for me," my daughter said at seventeen, "I can try stuff." At sixty-plus, time often seems to be going against me. Certainly it's going too fast. And certainly it can be a cruel bully, grief and devastation in the wake of every rampage.

How to live with the implacable? So far, my best recourse is to believe that I, too, can try stuff. Find fresh ways to be there, each and every day. Getting there, it has begun to seem clear, will happen all by itself, no need to lift a single finger.